Man's Subtle Bodies and Centres

the Aura, the Solar Plexus, the Chakras...

Translated from the French
Original title: CENTRES ET CORPS SUBTILS

Omraam Mikhaël Aïvanhov

Man's Subtle Bodies and Centres
the Aura, the Solar Plexus, the Chakras...

4th edition

Izvor Collection — No. 219

P R O S V E T A

Prosveta S.A – B.P.12 – 83601 Fréjus CEDEX (France)

ISSN: 0763-2738
ISBN 2-85566-383-0
édition originale: ISBN 2-85566-310-5

TABLE OF CONTENTS

1

HUMAN EVOLUTION
AND THE DEVELOPMENT
OF THE SPIRITUAL ORGANS

Every human being possesses a physical body which is made up of different organs. Even tiny children know that: ask them where their eyes are and they'll show you; or ask them to show you their mouth, their ears, their nose, their little legs and they'll delight in pointing to them. Later on, when they go to school they learn that man possesses five senses: sight, smell, hearing, taste and touch, and that each of these five senses has its own specific function; that the function and sensations of the sense of touch, for instance, are not the same as those of sight, taste or hearing, and so on.

All of man's contacts with his environment are based on his five senses and it is for this reason that he seeks to make the most of them and exploit all their possibilities; this is why, especially, he is constantly trying to enhance and vary the sensations his eyes, ears, skin, etc. can afford him. The various sensations experienced by men through the medium of their senses differ considerably in importance as well as in intensity. Take the question of taste, for instance: who can deny the wealth and variety of the sensations provided by the sense of taste when one treats oneself to a particularly delicious meal? Or take the sense of touch: when a man and woman caress each other they experience very intense sensations. In fact it is often thought that the most intense sensations are those provided by sexual pleasure, but this is not at all certain. It may be true, in general, but it is not true for everybody. Certain artists endowed with very great sensitivity of sight or hearing are far more deeply moved by colours and sounds than by the sexual act, which may even leave them indifferent and unmoved.

But as the majority of human beings are not so highly evolved as that, we can truthfully say that the two senses which govern the world today are those of touch (which includes sexuality) and taste. The senses of sight, hearing and smell seem to be relatively unimportant. In fact some people are totally indifferent to scents, sounds and colours unless their personal interests are involved, just as animals have developed a very keen sense of smell, sight and hearing because they need these senses for their own protection and in order to find food.

You know all this, already, of course, I realize that; but I mention it in order to draw your attention to certain conclusions that have certainly never occurred to you. For thousands of years men have been doing all they can to increase the variety and intensity of the sensations and perceptions transmitted by their five senses, and it is this play on the keyboard of man's five senses which they call culture and civilization. Well, all I can say is that I find this very inadequate! However great the degree of refinement of the five senses they will always be severely limited because they belong to the physical dimension and can never reach farther than the purely physical and explore what lies beyond.

Nature has planned other keys for this keyboard: yes, a sixth and even a seventh and eighth sense, far more intense and far more powerful. At the moment, though, men confine themselves to the use of their five physical senses: they refuse even to acknowledge that there are other dimensions waiting to be explored, other sights, scents and textures to be experienced. So it is not at all surprising that they are unable to enjoy new and more varied, richer or more subtle sensations. How can you explain the fact that whilst depriving their five physical senses of nourishment, some people have perceptions which put them into transports of delight: the scope of their consciousness is broadened and they experience an impression of fulfilment, majesty and immensity?

Human beings must realize that if they keep trying to multiply and amplify their physical sensations they are doomed to bitter disappointment, for these sensations are severely limited. Why? Because each organ is specialized: it has a specific function and can provide only those sensations which correspond to that function. If we want to experience fresh sensations we shall have to turn to other organs: organs which, although we don't know it, we all possess.

Observe the behaviour of human beings: they can look at whatever they please, they can taste or touch or buy whatever they like and yet they always feel that something is lacking. Why? Because they don't know that in order to feel fulfilled and enjoy the extraordinarily rich and powerful sensations they hunger for, they are going to have to stop relying exclusively on their five physical senses. In this respect Orientals are capable of experiences that would be utterly impossible for Westerners. In India or Tibet, for instance, there are yogis who live in holes in the ground. In darkness and complete silence the senses are deprived of all nourishment, and by constant meditation the yogi reduces them to a state of numbness. When the senses cease their activity, they no longer absorb the psychic energy intended for the subtle force-centres; these centres are awakened and the yogi begins to see, hear, smell and touch the fluidic elements of higher realms of reality. And this is why these exceptional human beings do everything in their power — some of them, for years on end — to suppress all visual, auditory and olfactory sensations and to eliminate all movement. The only activity left to them is that of thought and, eventually, they even cease all mental activity in order to live in total communion with the Deity.

God has endowed the human soul with certain latent faculties, but someone whose life is too absorbed by the things around him can prevent these faculties from developing. What do you do when you want to meditate, for example? Don't you close your eyes in order to turn all your attention inwards? Incidentally, while we're on the subject, let me mention something: when you meditate, don't keep your eyes closed for too long at a time, otherwise, as you are not Indian yogis yet, you are liable to fall asleep. Open your eyes briefly from time to time, without letting yourself be distracted by your surroundings, then close them and open them again, later. It is certainly advisable to close one's eyes when meditating because this helps one to shut out

one's surroundings and concentrate on one's
meditation, but if you keep your eyes closed for
too long sleep creeps up on you!

That's the way it is: when you open your eyes
you wake up and when you close them you are
preparing to sleep. It is a pattern which has been
etched into the brain for millions of years, and
when Nature, always faithful and true, sees you
closing your eyes, she says, 'You're closing your
eyes? You're sleepy? Well, we'll soon fix that!'
and before you know it she has plunged you into a
state of profound 'meditation'! When you open
your eyes, on the other hand, it is the signal that
it's time to wake up: everything comes to life, the
motor starts to hum, the brain, the arms and legs
all begin to stir. Yes, just one little movement —
your eyelids which flutter open — and a world of
activity is set in motion!

This question of opening or closing one's
eyes is very important. Sometimes someone will
tell you, 'Open your eyes!' But this is a manner of
speaking because your eyes were already open;
what do they mean? What eyes are they talking
about? There are other eyes which see more clearly, which have a far deeper, more spiritual vision.
The eyes of your physical body may be open but
you possess other eyes and they are still shut.
From time to time, however, one realizes that they
do exist and that it is possible to open them.

But in order to open one's spiritual eyes, the eyes which see the subtler aspects of reality, one has to close one's physical eyes. And then, at other moments the exact opposite is true: when you close your physical eyes your spiritual eyes close too, and when you open your physical eyes you open your spiritual eyes at the same time. As you see, there are some very subtle distinctions to be made here and, little by little, you will begin to distinguish them more clearly and use them in your daily lives.

Westerners have honed the life of the five senses to a high degree of perfection and they are convinced that that is the way to know all there is to know and to attain happiness! They know a great deal, that's true, and they experience a wide variety of sensations, but their five senses devour every drop of psychic energy so that they have none left for the spiritual dimension. In the West, people live too much in their physical sensations; they have no energy to spare for the cultivation of other faculties. Too many sensations! 'At least we're alive!' you might say. Yes, to be sure, you're alive. But it's a life which conceals the true life. It is important that you understand this and that you eliminate from your lives many different sensations which prevent you from perceiving things as they really are.

The use of drugs is more and more widespread today. People try to escape from the insipid monotony of their everyday lives with the help of opium, hashish, marijuana, cocaine and heroin. These drugs produce certain sensations of clairvoyance, clairaudience and so on, which give the user the illusion of having reached a higher state of consciousness. But it is only an illusion: in the long run they lose even their ordinary intellectual faculties and ruin their health. Although these drugs have been used for hundreds of years in the East and in South America they are obviously inadvisable. They are extremely harmful to the nervous system.

Hindus and Tibetans know a great deal about plants; the science has been handed down from one generation to the next for thousands of years. If you eat certain plants, apparently, they will enable you to survive for weeks without food, others will enable you to spend days and nights in the snows of the Himalayas without suffering from the cold. At least, so I have heard; I haven't tried them for myself, but it is quite possible. I believe in the power of herbs. There are also certain very potent herbal preparations which can be used to produce visions or astral projection. There are books in which one can read of how witches in the Middle Ages knew the secret of certain ointments or salves with which they smeared their bodies before taking part in the Sabbath. In fact it was not their physical bodies which took part in the Sabbath but their astral bodies. A few doctors have managed to get hold of some of these recipes and experimented with them, and they have found that the phenomena they describe are absolutely authentic. Of course, it is very difficult to be sure of reproducing the exact formula because they are never very clearly described, but all these ointments contained certain stimulants capable of inducing astral projection.

But enough of this for the moment. I mention these things simply to show you that there are extremely potent products which can give access to planes higher and more subtle than the physical, but that these products are often extremely dangerous. For this reason I advise you never to use them. The best method is to seek the sensations of fulfilment, freedom, buoyancy, joy and delight that you yearn for, by purely spiritual means. True disciples don't rely on external props, they know that God has placed all they need within them: gold and every other gift of Nature. All the products of all the laboratories and pharmaceutical companies of the world exist in abundance within themselves. All they have to do is fetch them out and use them. Wouldn't it be a pity if you spent ten or twenty years in an Initiatic School without ever learning to exploit your inner resources?

Each of our sense organs provides us with a partial knowledge of the world, and it is interesting to note the hierarchy that exists amongst them. The sense of touch is concerned principally with solids. One cannot feel gaseous or etheric matter at all and liquids only to a certain extent: the sense of touch specializes in solid, tangible realities. The sense of taste concerns what is liquid. If you object that a piece of toffee is solid enough, but that when it is in your mouth you can certainly taste it, I would have to tell you that you haven't studied the question very well: you can only taste what is in your mouth if it is being melted and liquified by your saliva. And what about the sense of smell? This sense allows us to perceive odours, that is, gaseous emanations. So the nose is also concerned with matter but it is matter of a subtler nature, for its particles float in the air. When we come to the sense of hearing we find that it is no longer concerned with matter but with waves and vibrations. The same is true of the sense of sight: sight brings us to the threshold of the etheric world. So this is how the senses are graded, as it were, hierarchically, ranging from the densest to the most subtle.

Now, if we want to penetrate into the astral world we can no longer rely on our five senses, we need another sense especially adapted for the purpose and capable of perceiving even subtler forms of matter. Anyone who has not developed this sixth sense cannot even be aware that there are other levels of matter, other regions. He never imagines that the universe is threaded through with other vibrations which can afford sensations far vaster and more intense than those known to him. If we want to touch something we have to be very close to it; to taste something, even more so. We can smell the scent of a flower from a certain distance; sounds can travel quite a long way to us, and we can see things which are even farther away, for our eyes are fashioned in such a way as to enable us to receive information and instructions from very far. As you can see, with marvellous intelligence, nature has established this hierarchy amongst the five senses. But her work did not stop there: other senses must now put us in touch with vaster and more remote regions of the universe.

Until man has developed the organs designed to put him in touch with more exalted entities in higher, subtler regions, his knowledge will be severely limited. He may talk, write, explain, criticize and pronounce judgment, but he will always be in error because he will know only one side of reality. If he wants to grasp the whole of reality he must practise until he suceeds in awakening other faculties which have always been there, within him, but which are still asleep, waiting until he is ready to use them. In the far distant past, when man had not fully taken possession of his physical body, Initiatic tradition tells us that he lived mainly out of his body, in a state of astral projection. Later on, when his spirit began to penetrate more deeply into matter, he developed the faculties which enabled him to work on the material level (the five senses) and he neglected his mediumistic faculties. But he did not lose these faculties; he still possesses them.

Observe the attitude of children: up to the age of about seven they are still not wholly present in their physical bodies. They reflect the period during which humanity as a whole was at that stage of evolution. At that time men spoke with nature spirits and the souls of the dead, they were in touch and communicated with them and, when they themselves came to die they did not know whether they were alive or dead. The Invisible World, the spirit world, was the reality that was most apparent and most important to them. They floated in the atmosphere as though they were immaterial and only entered their physical bodies every now and then. In these conditions they were totally unprepared to work in the material dimension. The evolutionary process, however, demanded that they penetrate this dimension. Modern man is equipped with formidable intellectual powers which enable him to dominate matter but he has lost something else : he has forgotten the very existence of the spiritual world; he has completely lost touch with it. Some, of course, still remember. They still have an intuition of the spiritual dimension, but the majority has forgotten.

There are two forms of knowledge, intellectual and spiritual and, of course, the best way is to develop both at the same time. We must not forget that Nature, that is to say Cosmic Intelligence, has Its own views on the subject of evolution. Its plan is for man to develop in both dimensions, in the material as well as in the spiritual dimension, but as it is very difficult to develop in two directions at once, It has allowed him to develop in only one direction for centuries and millenaries while, at the same time, keeping certain avenues open so as not to render him incapable of spiritual growth in the future. At this stage of their evolution, therefore, Cosmic Intelligence has decreed that human beings should develop in the area of physical sensations: sight, hearing, taste, touch, etc. Man must penetrate to the very heart of matter in order to touch it, explore and get to know it, in order to possess it and, above all, to work on it and fashion it.

You need not be surprised : that's the way it is, and it is only a phase. The human mind is obliged to penetrate ever deeper into matter in order to know it perfectly, and during this phase almost every trace of the heavenly homeland which was his in the distant past is wiped from his memory. But as he gets to know material reality more intimately he enriches himself in many ways and, above all, he begins to acquire dominion over his own matter. So far, of course, only a tiny minority is capable of this, but the goal of man's earthly existence is to penetrate so completely into his physical body that he is able to take full possession of all his faculties and use them to work on the world around him.

When I say that man's spirit has to 'penetrate into matter', I mean, first and foremost, that he has to enter fully into his own physical body, take possession of it and become its master. Once he is really and truly at home within his body, then he may work and exercise his influence on his environment. And here, too, he acts as one who dominates: transforming, building or destroying. This is the all-important phase of involution, of the descent into matter. But the Holy Spirit has great plans in mind for the human race. He will not let us continue indefinitely on the downward path; He will not allow us to become totally enmeshed in matter, or to lose all contact with Heaven and forget our divine origin. As soon as man has attained a sufficient degree of self-mastery, of control of his brain, his members and all his faculties, as soon as he has understood the properties of the elements, then other influences, other forces and currents will begin to make themselves felt and mankind will be borne upwards once again. Gradually, he will recover the faculties he possessed in the distant past. Then he will know both matter and the spirit.

In the Book of Genesis it says that Adam and Eve ate the fruit of the Tree of the Knowledge of Good and Evil. This means that they were not content to know only the spirit, they wanted to descend onto the level of matter, also. So they began the downward journey and, in this way, through joys and sorrows, sickness and health, their main object of study for millions of years has been evil. They could have stayed in Paradise. They could have been content to eat the fruit of the Tree of Everlasting Life. But curiosity got the better of them and they wanted to see what it was like down below, and it was this that led them to suffer from the cold, darkness, sickness and death.

And humanity is still on the downward path. Some religions call this downward path 'Original Sin', but it can also be interpreted as the choice of a certain course of studies. Yes, when they ate the fruit of the Tree of the Knowledge of Good and Evil, man embarked on a course of studies, and a very difficult course it is, for it requires him to confront a subject-matter which grows ever more dense. But what is wrong with that? Man wanted to descend in order to learn; he did so and now he is up to the ears in his studies and beginning to understand what kind of hell he has got himself into! So, for the moment he is studying Evil, but one fine day he will go back to where he came from and begin to study Good.

I know what Cosmic Intelligence has in mind, and I know that when human beings have learned to control and master matter, thanks to the work of their five senses, they will soar upwards again and start to develop their spiritual senses. All of you, therefore, who want to make progress on the path of evolution, should limit and reduce the sensations you receive through your five senses and start to look within your-selves. Your inner landscape is vast and very rich, but you have to search for its abundant treasures!

2

THE AURA

I

Everything that exists, be it human beings, animals, plants or even the stones in the ground, is surrounded by its own subtle, fluidic atmosphere made up of the particles and emanations it is constantly giving off. It is this atmosphere that constitutes the aura. Of course, it is not visible, except to clairvoyants and, in fact, a great many people don't even know that it exists. The aura is a kind of halo which surrounds every human being, the only difference being that some people's aura is immense and very brilliant, extending its gloriously varied colours and intense vibrations to great distances, whereas others are meagre and lustreless, with dirty, blurred colours.

The aura can be compared to the skin of our physical bodies and you all know how vital the skin is. It serves several important purposes, first amongst them being that of protection: like a shield or a suit of armour, it protects us against blows, sudden changes of temperature and so on. Another function of the skin is to serve as an organ of exchange: it breathes in and out, absorbing certain elements and eliminating others. And, finally, the skin serves as a sense organ which enables us to experience sensations of heat and cold, contact with other bodies, pain, and so on. But my intention is not to talk about the functions of the skin: that is not my concern. If you want to learn more about it you can look it up in anatomy and physiology books. What I am interested in today is in drawing a parallel between the skin and the aura.

The aura has exactly the same functions as the skin. You could say that it is the skin of the soul which it surrounds and protects. It is also its sense organ and, finally, it is the means of communication which enables the soul to receive the Cosmic currents flowing through space and to communicate and exchange with others, with other human souls, other creatures of the universe, even with the stars in the heavens, and with the Supreme Universal Soul.

On the other hand, the aura can be compared to the earth's atmosphere. Yes, the comparison is extraordinarily revealing! The earth is surrounded by a protective screen: its skin. The earth's skin, or atmosphere, is a great deal thicker than ours, that's true, but it serves exactly the same purpose. Who could ever say how many times the earth has escaped destruction during the course of its journey through space, thanks to its atmosphere? Think of all the meteors and particles, large and small, hurtling through space which would collide with our planet with catastrophic results if it were not for the atmosphere which causes them to burn up and disintegrate before they reach the earth! And the atmosphere protects us from still other dangers; certain cosmic rays, for instance, which would be deadly for us if they were not neutralized by chemical elements contained in the different layers of the atmosphere.

Thanks to our aura, therefore, we benefit from a continuing relationship of reciprocal exchange with the forces of nature. The cosmic, planetary and zodiacal influences ceaselessly flowing through space reach out to touch us and, depending on the purity and sensitivity of our aura and the colours it contains, we may capture or fail to capture certain specific forces. Our aura, therefore, is like an antenna, it is an instrument which detects and receives messages, waves and forces coming to us from the length and breadth of the universe. Now, suppose there are certain negative, harmful influences at large in the universe: if your aura is very powerful and very luminous, those negative influences will be unable to reach your consciousness or to upset or harm you. Why? Because before they can get to you they come up against your aura, and your aura is an impenetrable barrier. It is like a wall or, if you prefer, like a customs house at the frontier between two countries, and the customs officers on duty allow no one through without first inspecting their trunks, suitcases and handbags. These customs officers act without your being aware of it, but they can warn you of danger. So, as you see, although we distinguish the different functions of the aura, in practice they are closely linked: sensitivity, exchange and protection all function at once.

Now, let's look at the factors which contribute to the quality of our aura. They are exactly the same as those which influence the quality of our skin. There are different types of skin: coarse-grained, rough and dry or, on the contrary, smooth, fine-grained and soft. Almost anyone can judge the quality of a person's skin at a glance, but what gives the skin its particular qualities? The overall physical and psychic condition of the person's organism. Man makes his own skin.

Yes, indeed! A person's skin reveals a great deal about its owner. If it is really fine and spiritual it shows that he is a spiritual person, for the skin a person makes for himself cannot lie, it necessarily corresponds to what he is. Of course, man is unaware that he is responsible for making his own skin. In fact, if he knew how, he could even change the skin he now has. This is very difficult, of course, but it is possible — and it is very important. Man's entire destiny depends on his skin because it has a determining influence on his relations with other human beings and with the world at large. I am telling you this today because I want you to think about it. Every detail of your skin has significance. Its consistence (whether it is smooth and supple, hard, flabby or soft) reflects your essential qualities and characteristics: perseverance, willpower and activity or frailty, laziness and failings.

The whole of a man's destiny, all his triumphs and all his failures, are expressed in his skin. Greet someone with a handshake and you already have some idea of the essential traits of his character. And if you knew exactly what the physical characteristics corresponded to, you would only have to shake hands with him once to have a detailed and accurate picture of his strengths and weaknesses. But as people shake hands automatically, without paying attention to what they're doing, they never learn anything. We shake someone's hand in order to make contact, to establish a relationship of exchange in which we must give some of the good that is in us and receive the same from them. If there is nothing to be gained from the gesture, we might as well not do it at all.

But let's get back to the subject of the aura. As I told you a moment ago, the aura is formed by our emanations, and not only the emanations of the physical body: those would not be sufficient. The aura is far more complex than that, it is a combination of all the emanations of all our subtle bodies, each of which, by adding its own unique emanations adds its own shades and tints to the whole. A man's etheric body forms an aura which penetrates and interweaves with the aura of his physical body and the combined aura of his physical and etheric bodies reveals the state of his health and vigour. His astral and mental bodies, according to their activity or inertia, their qualities or their weaknesses, add their own special emanations, their own colouring, to the initial aura, thus revealing the nature of his thoughts and feelings. And if the causal, buddhic and atmic bodies have been awakened, they add yet other, brighter, more luminous colours and other, more powerful vibrations.

It is these emanations of the three higher bodies of man which form the Body of Glory of which Saint Paul speaks in his Epistles. I have often mentioned this before. It is also called the Body of Immortality, the Body of Light or the Body of Christ. When Jesus was transfigured on Mount Thabor he appeared to Peter, James and John, accompanied by Moses and Elijah, and such brilliance radiated from him that his disciples fell flat on their faces, unable to bear it. The Gospel says, 'His face shone like the sun, and his clothes became as white as the light.' This transfiguration was a manifestation of Jesus' Body of Glory.

The Body of Glory, like the aura, is an emanation of a human being, but whereas the aura expresses the whole man — his faults as well as his virtues — his Glorious Body expresses only the most intense level of his spiritual life. This is why only the great Masters manifest their Body of Glory. It is thanks to their Body of Glory, so pure and luminous, that they are able to heal the sick, bring blessings on people and places wherever they go and move freely through the vastness of space.

The aura, therefore, is a blend of all the different emanations of every aspect of a human being. This is why, when an Initiate wishes to know someone, he attaches far more importance

to his aura than to his outward appearance : phys-
iognomy, gestures or language. All those colours,
forces and fluidic emanations which escape from
a man and which he is powerless either to halt or
to hide — this is what an Initiate looks for. Some
people are past masters at camouflaging their
true characters ; they keep a careful check on their
voice, their gestures, looks and words. But what
they don't know is that they have no control over
the subtle manifestations of their inner life. Their
thoughts and feelings create forms and colours,
and it is not in their power either to alter or to con-
ceal them. This is why a true Initiate sees through
outward appearances : he knows immediately if
someone is living in harmony or disorder, if he
emanates something constructive and beneficial
which communicates life and light, an atmosphere which strengthens and purifies or if, on
the contrary, he is bogged down, a prisoner of his
lower self. Even the state of one's health can be
assessed from the aura for the state of one's
organs, the liver, lungs, brain and so on, is
reflected in the aura.

So the aura is a book, but a book so subtle
that it is difficult to have any notion of it. And
just as there are no two human beings with identical fingerprints, so there are no two human
beings whose auras are exactly alike, for the aura
represents the whole human being.

The earth's atmosphere is permeated with the emanations of human beings, animals, plants, rocks, water, mountains and all the forces flowing from the planets and the stars. And the human aura reflects this: it is a vast and very rich synthesis of all that is in man. As I have said, minerals, plants and animals also have an aura, but theirs is a purely physical aura. Minerals, metals and crystals give off certain forces which form a sort of miniature magnetic field of colour around them.

The aura of plants is more intense and has more vitality than that of minerals because their etheric body adds its own vigour, its own compelling urge for growth. The aura of animals is richer again, because animals have an astral body, the body of desire. In general, animals have not yet begun to develop their mental body, although it does seem that there are a few exceptions such as dogs, horses, elephants and monkeys, in which biologists detect a certain capacity for thought. A very rudimentary form of thought, of course, but thanks to their contact with men, animals can begin to develop their mental body. The care and affection human beings give their animals contribute greatly to their evolution. As for human beings, the development their mental body is undergoing at the moment is absolutely prodigious. True, it doesn't always develop in the right

direction, but those who know how to guide and
control their thought strengthen their auras
tremendously.

Then there are the Saints, Prophets and
Initiates: their attitude of adoration and their
love for the Creator make their causal, buddhic
and atmic bodies grow and develop into an aura
of dazzling splendour in which the colours swirl
and flow in ceaseless movement, like a glorious
display of fireworks. The aura of a Master is
immense; in fact we are told that Buddha's aura
extended for several leagues. Yes, a great Master
can reach out so far with his aura that he can take
a whole region under his protection and, at the
same time, penetrate and intermingle with the
aura of those who live in that region, breathing
new life into them. A Master's dearest wish is to
spread his aura farther and farther, to reach and
'take under his wing' the greatest possible number of human beings. This is his ideal, an ideal of
sublime nobility! By means of his aura a Master
purifies the atmosphere around him, illuminating and giving new life and a new beauty to all
creatures. It is through his aura, also, that he is
able to influence plants and their seeds and even
alter atmospheric currents. Yes, indeed! The aura
of an Initiate is truly divine!

Thanks to the immensity of their aura which
enables them to reach many remote regions of the

universe, Initiates acquire a profound grasp of things which is not a purely intellectual understanding. This is why I tell you that you must stop applying your minds to all kinds of concerns which will give you neither happiness nor celestial visions, and launch out on the wings of your strong, luminous aura, towards the sublime heights where you may learn how God created the world and what messages He has left inscribed on the stars and the mountains, on lakes, birds, animals and plants. But most vital of all, the essential condition for enhancing the intensity, purity and power of your aura, is that you have the lofty ideal of working towards your own perfection, of doing only what is just and noble, of harbouring only the purest thoughts and feelings.

Those who maintain that the nature of their thoughts, feelings and actions is totally irrelevant, that we have to free ourselves from antiquated religious and moral codes, are destroying the beauty of their aura and produce only dull, dirty colours and chaotic vibrations and, without knowing why, other people sense this and tend to avoid them. People are only drawn to what is pure, luminous and harmonious, and if someone wants others to like him he has to understand that he must allow only pure, luminous forces into his inner being. For those who desire love, light and power there is one way, and only one, of achieving their heart's desire, and that is to work hard to cleanse their aura of all the impure colours whose bad vibrations destroy the good in others. You have all experienced this, surely: some people can be with you only five minutes and, when they go, you find yourself sucked dry of all inspiration: all joy, all faith in God have left you. Everything bright and good has vanished! But there are others: after only a few minutes in their presence you feel that your life is renewed, your old, worn-out cells have been replaced by new ones, and once again you are full of faith and energy. You have to understand that it is their aura which causes the changes in you.

This explains how the aura can be an instrument of magic in the hands of an Initiate. Since it is an integral part of his being, wherever an Initiate goes his presence benefits the mineral, vegetable, animal and human reigns. But that is not all, for a Master can even use his aura to help the billions upon trillions of disembodied beings in space. Yes, his aura can even reach out to help beings there, in the other world. I know all about this question; I have given it much study. A Master is constantly at work to improve the lot of countless beings in the astral and mental worlds. Even though, on earth, he may take care of only a handful of human beings, on the other side he is always in contact with a multitude of creatures who gather round him to receive warmth, light and renewed life from his aura in order to advance their evolution.

Yes, the veritable field of action of the great Masters is not here on earth, amongst human beings. Although it cannot be seen by human eyes, their most intense activity takes place on the other side. The great Masters who, with all their hearts, souls and minds, have fully achieved their ideal of serving God, have awakened their causal and buddhic bodies, and it is the vibrations of these sublime bodies which reach even those who dwell on other planets. In the same way, Masters who dwell on other planets reach the creatures of earth, and in this way there is a continual flow of exchange, not only within our solar system, but throughout the length and breadth of the whole cosmos. God has placed no boundaries or frontiers in the universe and if it is true to say that love is all-powerful it is because love can reach to the stars and touch even the most remote and far-distant entities.

Why do you suppose that the saints were traditionally portrayed with halos circling their heads? There was once an elaborate science of colour in the past, which taught that each virtue was expressed by a particular colour and that the colours produced by these virtues formed the aura. The saints are beings of great purity whose overriding desire is to draw ever closer to God, to melt into Him in order to know Him and become as He is, and because of this burning desire to know God they acquire such deep insight and such great wisdom, that golden yellow light flows from their innermost being and folds them in its glory. There are all sorts of different shades of yellow ranging from the palest, most delicate tints to a strong golden yellow. Each shade and tint has its own special meaning and there is a great deal that could be said about this subject, for it touches on an alchemical question: the question of how to transform matter into fluidic gold.

If a disciple fails to protect himself by the development of certain inner qualities and virtues, enemies will steal into him and he will not be able to get rid of them again. What should he do, therefore, to defend himself? He should work to develop the purity, brightness, beauty, power and magnitude of his aura. Each one of these aspects depends on the virtues he cultivates. If a man is pure his aura becomes limpid and transparent; if he is intelligent it becomes brighter and more luminous; if his life is very intense his aura vibrates, too, with great intensity; if he has developed his willpower it becomes very powerful, and if he has concentrated all his energies on spiritual things his aura expands and grows until it becomes immense. And the beauty of the aura, that is the beauty of its colours, depends on the harmony which reigns amongst all its different qualities and virtues. There are many more subtle distinctions and shades of difference in the aura, but I have given you the essential points.

Those who always think good thoughts, therefore, those who possess faith, hope, kindness and purity, share in the wealth of nature, and evil can no longer penetrate their defences. They are protected as though by a shield. In fact, the shield with which the knights in fairy tales defend themselves is a symbol of their aura. And the sword? The sword represents the rays of light radiating from man. The aura is the protective screen which surrounds us: it represents the feminine principle; and man's thought or spirit darting out into space, represents the masculine, active, dynamic principle. So these two symbols, sword and shield, which can be traced back to the earliest ages of mankind, represent the two principles: the feminine principle, the aura, and the active masculine principle, man's thought sustained by his will, which flashes out from him like an arrow. As we know, the sword, arrow or spear has always been seen as the symbol of the active masculine principle. In astrology, the figure of Sagittarius shooting his arrows into the air is a symbol of the Initiate who draws his bow and shoots his thoughts, his mental arrows, in defence of the city of the Initiates, to prevent his enemies from entering.

All around us we see examples of how, on the physical level, human beings have perfected the tools and appliances they use for work or defence. Vacuum cleaners have taken the place of brooms, tractors have replaced horse-drawn carts, tanks, rockets and missiles have replaced the arrows, lances and bayonets of the past. But on the spiritual level human beings are still poor and under-equipped. And yet all sorts of tools and weapons are available. Everything that has been discovered on the physical level has its equivalent on the spiritual level. On the physical level our bodies are protected by our skin and clothes; on the spiritual level we are protected by our aura.

There is no more effective protection than a pure, luminous aura. Of course, all the magic objects, figures and formulas enumerated in esoteric tradition have value and their own profound meaning. But no formula, no talisman is as powerful as the aura. Before calling on the spirits — especially before evoking spirits of darkness — a Magus draws a circle round himself in which he inscribes the names of God or certain symbols. This circle represents the aura. No man can command the spirits of darkness with impunity if he is not surrounded by a strong protective circle, a powerful aura. And speaking in a general way, too, one may say that no one can ever achieve substantial spiritual results if he is not surrounded by a protective circle, if, in other words, his aura is not composed of all those divine forces and virtues symbolized by the names of God inscribed in the magic circle.

A great many people dabble in magic without knowing the origin of the symbols they use or the real meaning of what they are doing. They are content to perform the rites according to instructions in their book, oblivious of the fact that it is within themselves that they should trace a circle and inscribe the names of God, that it is they themselves who must acquire the virtues that will ensure an aura of purity, holiness, light and love. They don't know this and so, in spite of the magic circle, they remain highly vulnerable. The circle they draw exists only on the outside; on the inside they do not have the qualities they need, so they are not protected.

When you hear that a Magus places himself inside a circle, with a sword or wand in his hand, and reads a formula out of a book, it is all perfectly true. But, for an Initiate, each detail of a rite corresponds to something he already possesses in himself. First of all, an Initiate must possess his own inner magic wand, his inner sword, and his own inner book of formulas. An Initiate reads from a book and the book represents his inner knowledge of all the forces and all the spirits of nature. The magic wand or sword represents the inflexible willpower with which he must work. If he doesn't possess that wand it means that he doesn't possess the willpower he needs and he will be unable to command the spirits.

Now, how should you go about this work on your aura? There are two ways. The first is by a deliberate, conscious effort, by concentrating mentally on colour. Picture yourself bathed in the purest, most luminous colours. A prism can be a great help in this by giving you an accurate idea of the seven colours, for those one sees in nature, in flowers or birds, for instance, are never exactly the colours of sunlight. Whereas with a prism you can see the true colours: red, orange, yellow, green, blue and purple. Then you can imagine that you see all these colours flowing out from you and spreading throughout space; picture yourself bathed in that light, in all those glorious colours; imagine that you are surrounded by a luminous sphere and that you are sending your love out into the whole wide universe. One can get so much delight from exercises like this that it is quite possible that once you have begun you will never want to stop!

The other method for working on your aura is by concentrating all your efforts on acquiring the virtues of purity, patience, forbearance, generosity, hope, faith, humility, justice and disinterestedness. This second method is certainly the safest: your work is to cultivate these virtues and it is they that form your aura. Of course, you can combine both methods, and that is even better. If you cultivate the virtues your aura will develop naturally; or you can develop it by means of a conscious work of the imagination, but this is the less effective way. Suppose, for example, that you concentrated on your aura every day but that, at the same time, you continued to live a very ordinary life, breaking many of the divine laws: on the one hand you would be building something lovely but, on the other, you would be destroying what you build. So it is far better to combine the two methods: live an honest life in purity and love and, at the same time, use your imagination consciously to cultivate your aura.

As I have already told you, as your aura grows and spreads it will enable you to communicate with every area of the universe. If you study the planets of our solar system you will see that, although they are millions of miles apart, yet they touch each other, they are all joined to form a whole. Yes, if we think that they are separated from each other it is because we see only the

outward, visible appearances. Take the earth, for
example : the continents take up a certain amount
of space but the oceans cover more of the earth's
surface than the land. The atmosphere, that layer
of gaseous matter surrounding the earth, on the
other hand, is several times the volume of the
planet. Then beyond the earth's atmosphere is its
etheric body and, beyond that again, its astral
and mental bodies which are even more
voluminous. For the earth is a living, intelligent
being which also has a soul and a spirit. And as
this is also true of the other planets you can see
how they all intermingle and penetrate each
other. Their physical bodies are very far from
each other, but their auras and emanations touch
and join. This explains the planetary influences
known to astrology : by means of their auras, the
planets penetrate and act upon each other and
upon those who inhabit them.

There are still many aspects of the aura
which I have not explained, but what really matters is that you learn to care for your aura just as
you care for your skin. You have a bath or shower
and wash yourself, don't you? Of course! But
when it comes to the aura it's a little more compli-
cated : you can't apply lotions or creams — or raw
steak — to make it smooth and velvety! Besides,
all those things are not much good for your skin,
either. Some women never wash their face, for

instance, in the belief that it is bad for the skin. But there is nothing better than water! Forget about all those creams and lotions. They can even be dangerous: you never know what can get into you through your pores.

Humanity today is used to doing everything possible to improve the outward appearance of things, but in the future people will attach more importance to the inner reality and, instead of running to earthly beauty salons, women will go to their own 'spiritual beauty salons', by which I mean that they will cultivate and care for their aura. For the aura is the only authentic beauty salon. An intense, luminous aura bestows beauty on its owner, and it has at least this advantage: it is a beauty that lasts! A woman who has just been through the mill in a beauty salon may come out looking a perfect picture, but twenty-four hours later she'll look more like a 'genuine antique'! And the reason is simply that the improvement in her looks didn't come from within: if it doesn't come from within it can't last.

The particles emanating from a great Master are alive, intense, luminous and potent. When they penetrate our aura they enter into our very structure and transform our whole being. Those who receive their Master's emanations with loving hearts begin to think and to behave like him and, one day, they become as free as he is. This does not happen at once, of course; it takes years and years, but it does happen. Unfortunately people are not interested in what is invisible. They trust only what they can see or touch. They neglect the unseen aspects of reality completely. And yet that aspect is so important!

Make up your minds, therefore, to cultivate your aura and you will find that you are beginning to understand many things. When you are angry you are steeped in a fiery red, a dark, dirty red, very unlike the rosy red of love. And if you are lacking in faith, if you are not at peace in yourself, you will have a dull, ugly shade of blue in your aura, whereas, as your faith becomes stronger the blue of your aura becomes a brighter and brighter sky blue.

And now, here is an exercise which you should try to do every day: take a prism and hold it up so that the sun's rays strike it and observe how the white light of the sun is refracted into seven true colours as it passes through the prism. Then, when you have gazed at the colours for a little while, close your eyes and imagine that you are surrounded by purple, then blue, green, yellow and so on. Or, if you prefer, start with red and follow through in reverse order, holding each colour wrapped round you as it were, for several minutes. If you do this exercise every day, it will purify and strengthen your aura and you'll be amazed to find yourself in splendid form. Also, if a friend or someone in your family falls ill or is unhappy and discouraged, if you really want to help them, do the same exercise for them. Send them some of those beautiful colours of the prism. Oh, yes! There are a great many ways in which you can use the aura and the seven colours.

You can do all these exercises with light and colour when you go up to watch the sunrise in the morning. Looking at the sun and its aura and all the colours pouring from it into space, say to yourself, 'I want to be like the sun. I, too, want to be surrounded by rays of golden light' — or blue or purple or green light, as you please. And then, spend a long time steeping yourself in the splendour of those colours; contemplate them, picture them reaching out far, far away, so that every living creature is bathed in this marvellous atmosphere, swimming in light, drenched in light — and your aura will be a blessing for all creatures. This is possible. There are no limits to what you can do; it is human beings who impose limits on themselves. Your ambition for good must know no limits. Promise yourself, 'I'll do it; I'll get there!' A Master, or a disciple who is already very advanced, radiates love to the whole of creation, to the whole universe. Their love reaches out beyond the stars. Yes, indeed! It's true: some send their love as far as the stars, and the stars send back a floodtide of love which breaks over them like an ocean wave carrying all before it, and they find themselves swimming in love. Cosmic love is their very environment.

II

One of the functions of the aura is to permit communication and exchange between the planets and stars outside us and those within us. If our aura is impure and clouded, not only will it be unreceptive to the beneficial currents from the heavens, but it will attract harmful ones. It is often said that certain planets are benefic while others are malefic. But if this is so how do we explain the fact that a particular planet may have a favourable influence on some and an unfavourable influence on others? It is very simple: some people are receptive only to the negative currents of a planet: they cannot receive its positive currents. As a matter of fact, all the planets are benefic, but their influence on human beings depends on each person's aura. If someone's aura contains elements which resist and prevent beneficial planetary currents from entering, the currents are damaged and broken by this resistance and their effects become harmful. Whereas all influences, even harmful ones, become beneficial for someone whose aura is strong and pure.

There is nothing to be surprised about if I say that there are planets within man as well as in space! Man is a reflection of the cosmos, and all the planets exist within him and, like those we see in the universe, spin in orbit around his inner sun. A great deal could be said about this science which was known in the past but which has almost disappeared today. But one day, in the future, it will be known and taught again.

Mars, Saturn, Uranus and Pluto are considered malefic and, in fact, they are malefic for those who are unreceptive to their virtues. The good qualities of Mars are a strong will, fearlessness and resolution in overcoming difficulties and reaching one's goal; the negative aspects of Mars are, as you all know, cruelty, violence and the urge to be destructive. The good qualities of Venus are beauty, charm and thoughtfulness, and the negative aspects are sensuality, superficiality and infidelity. Human beings attract and manifest the good or the bad influences of these planets by affinity and depending on whether their aura is pure or, on the contrary, clouded by negative elements. The same rules apply to all the planets. It is the qualities in our own aura which attract the virtues of Saturn (patience, stability, a thirst for knowledge) or his vices (melancholy, obstinacy and bitterness). Similarly we can attract Jupiter's virtues (greatness of soul, generosity, kindness, clemency) or his vices (ambition, vanity, the will to dominate and even crush others). The whole question, therefore, for a disciple, is to learn how to cultivate and develop his aura so that it may attract only favourable influences from the planets. For, contrary to the opinion of most astrologers, the good or evil influence of the planets does not depend exclusively on a person's Sign, the Houses in which the planets are placed or their aspects. The planetary influence will manifest itself very differently depending on the different degrees of evolution of the persons concerned. It is true, therefore, to say that 'the stars influence man but do not determine him'.

As you can see, the aura is extremely important. If your aura is not pure you cannot benefit either from the good influences of the planets or from the countless blessings which the angelic world is constantly showering on us, because your true self is buried and hidden under dense layers of impurities. We all know that a heavy layer of cloud hides the sun so that it can no longer warm or give light to creatures on earth. This is exactly what is wrong with those who live in anguish and distress, those who are filled with hatred and anger: there are too many dense clouds in their aura. The aura possesses an infinitely subtle variety of vibrations. It is constantly stirring with rapid movements, ceaselessly and faithfully reflecting the smallest changes in our state of mind and even in our physical condition. True, the aura is constant in that it always manifests the fundamental nature of its owner, but subtle variations flit through it continually. It is like a person's face: in the course of the day it registers every possible expression, but that doesn't mean that the shape of his nose, forehead or mouth have actually changed. Similarly with the aura: it is made up of certain radiations and colours which reveal a person's true nature, and this does not change substantially during his lifetime, but other, secondary vibrations come and go, reflecting transitory changes and states.

Those who give way to certain emotions or weaknesses, therefore, are constantly clouding the atmosphere of their aura, so that when beneficial currents and forces seek an entry, looking for a welcome and a place to rest, they come up against a barricade of muddy, opaque colours. If your life is meaningless and chaotic your aura will be crisscrossed by so many untidy eddies and currents that it will no longer be an effective shield against the hostility of invisible enemies. In these conditions you will be unable to establish a harmonious relationship of mutual exchange with the universe and other living creatures. In keeping with the Law of Affinity you will be receptive only to all that is sombre, chaotic and discordant in the universe; all that is luminous will automatically be rejected. Light attracts light; purity attracts purity. So if your aura is impure, muddy and chaotic all the pure, harmonious, luminous forces will keep away. Only those which are muddy and ugly will be able to get in because your aura only opens its doors to forces of the same breed as itself. Like to like. There is a proverb in Bulgaria which says that 'Mangy mules can smell each other seven hills away..' and they are eager to be in each other's company!

If your aura is not luminous, therefore, it is not an effective protection, nor is it a good instrument with which to receive signals from the Invisible World and perceive the hidden aspect of reality. This means that you will possess neither intuition nor foresight, nor be able to exchange messages with Heaven; entities dwelling in the far-away regions of space will not notice that you exist. Those who dwell in the sublime heights of the Invisible World will not even see you. Whereas if your aura is luminous they will see you perfectly. How? Well, suppose you are on a ship in the middle of the ocean at night; if your ship is not carrying any lights no one will be able to see it, but if you send up a flare or switch on a search-light, someone will see you at once and will be able to communicate with you. This is only an example, of course, because there are so many different means of communication nowadays, but it gives some idea of what I am trying to get you to understand.

The world is like an ocean and we are little ships sailing through the night. We are com-pletely in the dark, and if we don't switch on a light of some kind, invisible beings, Angels and Archangels, won't see us. So we have to send out beams of light, and it is our aura which does this. Someone who has a very luminous aura, therefore, can be seen by those who work in the heavenly spheres, and if he calls on them for help they can find him at once, thanks to the light of his aura. This, too, is no more than an illustration for, as you can well imagine, if the angelic spirits want to find someone they have more than one means at their disposal! The world has always been considered to be a 'vale of tears', suffering and darkness. Well, is it surprising that nobody notices when human beings cry out in pain, and groan and curse their fate? Is it any wonder that no one comes to their rescue? They don't produce any light! They have to send out signals of light, and the aura is the instrument that they should use for this purpose.

So your aura can serve to attract the attention of heavenly entities, but it can also give you access to the regions in which those entities dwell. When you want to visit certain places you need a special pass or visa. This is true on the physical plane and it is equally true on the spiritual plane. If you want permission to enter certain regions of the invisible world you must have a pass, and that pass is your aura: the colours of your aura. This means that in order to gain admittance to a particular region your aura must contain the special colours of that region. If, for instance, your aura is rich in golden yellow, you will be allowed into Nature's libraries and all her secrets will be revealed to you. The blue of your aura will take you to the region of music or religion; red will give you entry to the region in which you will find the very essence of vitality. So it is the quality of your aura which determines whether or not you gain admittance to the invisible world. The colours it contains are like so many passes for the corresponding regions, and the spiritual entities of those regions invite you in and come to your help.

But the condition and quality of the aura, its purity and transparency, depend on the way a person lives. If a man lets himself slide into an attitude of sloth and gives free rein to all kinds of disorders and vices, his aura becomes like a foul swamp and other people smell the nauseating stench arising from it. Even if they can't see anything — and it's very difficult to see someone's aura unless one is clairvoyant — they sense the presence of something dark and oppressive, like the atmosphere in the vicinity of a swamp. Whereas an Initiate or a Master who, for hundreds and even thousands of years has striven to develop the virtues of love, wisdom, purity and disinterestedness, possesses an immense aura in which innumerable creatures come and bask, and in which they feel nourished, soothed, strengthened and borne on towards a heavenly goal. This is why a Master's disciples can get great blessings from his aura as long as they are conscious of the fact; if their consciousness is not awakened to this reality, whatever he may do to help them they will be closed to his influence.

But a disciple must not be content to benefit from his Master's aura; he must also strive to develop his own, and in order to do this he must change his life. If he never does anything to change his mediocre way of life, with all its weaknesses and all its stupid contradictions, he can concentrate on his aura every day until he's blue in the face, but it won't do him much good. The situation is exactly the same when it comes to people's health: if they are content to take the medicines prescribed by their doctor and refuse to change the way of life that has made them ill, the medicines will never be more than a palliative. But it is very difficult to get human beings to see that the only really effective method is to change the way they live.

If your aura is pure it is you yourself who will be the first to benefit and be transformed by it, but it will also work changes in your environment, and this is why other people will begin to appreciate you. Without realizing why, they will feel happy and at ease when they are with you. In point of fact, what they feel is a presence, the presence of creatures of light that have been attracted by your aura. Heavenly entities are attracted by pure colours, so when they see someone surrounded by the light and colours they love they come flocking to him and, in the same way, entities of darkness cluster round evil, vicious people, rendering them repugnant to other people around them. But human beings are so unconscious, they have no idea why or how they attract good or evil to themselves.

The aura is a highly structured, hierarchically ordered world. Like the Tree of Life it is divided into regions in which dwell Angels, Archangels and benevolent Nature spirits, but it can also harbour diabolical spirits from Hell. It all depends on the life a person leads. He who is blessed with the presence of spirits of light manifests himself in extraordinary gifts of clairvoyance, clairaudience, healing and so on: he works miracles! Whereas when someone has attracted malicious entities we speak of possession or bewitchment.

It is clear, therefore, that we must work for years and years to improve ourselves and perfect our aura until it becomes an antenna capable of attracting all that is most beautiful and most beneficial in the universe. If I asked you, 'Are you really interested in good health, beauty, peace and happiness? Do you really want to be loved?' you would certainly reply, 'Yes, of course. That's all we want from life!' But if you really want these things so much why don't you do anything to get them? They won't just drop from Heaven, by chance. The best way to get them is to work at perfecting your aura: you can vivify it by your love, make it brighter and more luminous by your wisdom, strengthen it and make it powerful by your strength of character, and you can make it pure and translucid by the purity of your own life. The qualities with which you endow your aura entirely depend on the virtues you develop in yourself.

Don't think that if you develop just one virtue it will be enough to win you all the blessings you need. No, everything in the universe fits into a pattern and each virtue brings with it a corresponding blessing. It would take too long to explain all the different aspects of this, but think about it for yourselves. If you are observant you have almost certainly had the opportunity to notice this in some of the most ordinary events in life. Suppose you hear someone talking with tremendous conviction, and you see that the strength of his conviction is convincing others, then you start to analyse his words carefully and you realize that a lot of what he was saying simply didn't make sense. On the other hand you know people who think and speak very intelligently, but they never manage to convince others: nobody listens to them. The power of persuasion, you see, is one thing and intelligence is quite something else again! In the same way, different virtues in your Self will determine the different qualities of your aura. So, think about this and try to understand that it is only by working every day to endow your aura with new qualities that you will finally obtain all that your heart desires.

3

THE SOLAR PLEXUS

I

The sympathetic nervous system of man consists of a chain of nerve centres running from the brain to the base of the spinal cord, and a peripheral series of nerves and ganglia connected by a network of nerve-fibres known as plexuses. The solar plexus, located behind the stomach, is one of these.

Now, if you refer to Figure 1 on page 69, you will see that the ganglia of the sympathetic nerve system are grouped as follows:

Three pairs of cranial ganglia lying along the trigeminal nerve.

Three pairs of cervical ganglia connected to the heart.

Twelve pairs of dorsal ganglia connected to the lungs and the solar plexus.

Four pairs of lumbar ganglia which are also connected to the solar plexus and, thence, to the stomach, small intestine, liver, pancreas and kidneys.

Four pairs of sacral ganglia, connected to the rectum, the genital organs and the bladder.

This gives twenty-six pairs in all. And the number twenty-six is no mere chance: it is the sum of the four letters of the name of God, ה ו ה י (Yod He Vau He) in which Yod = 10, He = 5, Vau = 6, He = 5. What a wonderful thing that the name of God should be built according to the very same laws which govern the structure of man's sympathetic nerve system!

The two groups made up of three pairs of ganglia (cranial and cervical) are linked to the divine world and correspond to the psychological aspect of nature.

The twelve pairs of dorsal ganglia are linked to the spiritual world; they correspond to the physiological aspect of nature.

The two groups of four pairs of ganglia (lumbar and sacral) are linked to the physical dimension and correspond to the anatomical aspect of nature.

And now let's have a closer look at each of these groups (see Figure 2, page 71). First of all, we have two sets of three pairs of cranial ganglia: Three always stands for the Divinity; it is the number of the Cabbalah, for the Cabbalah reveals the factors, the active Principles

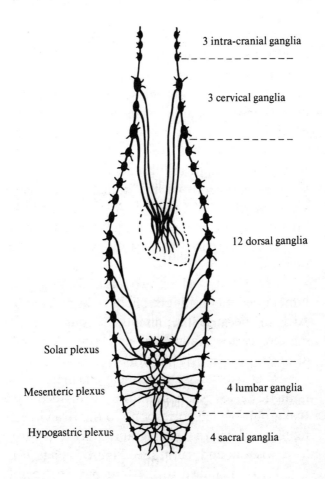

Figure 1. The chain of ganglia in the sympathetic nerve system.

in the universe. The Cabbalah answers the question, 'Who?'. Who creates? Who is at work in the universe?

Then there are twelve pairs of dorsal ganglia, and Twelve represents Nature ruled by the stars. It is the number of Astrology (the twelve Constellations of the Zodiac) which studies the influence of the heavenly bodies on men and the functions of the cosmic organs. Astrology is linked to our respiratory and circulatory systems. The Vernal Point, for example, retrogrades one degree every seventy-two years and the human heart beats seventy-two times a minute. Also, we normally breathe eighteen times in a minute; four times eighteen is seventy-two. Astrology answers the question, 'When?'.

And finally we have two sets of four pairs of lumbar and sacral ganglia; Four is the number of Alchemy because it represents the four states of matter, earth, water, air and fire. Alchemy answers the question 'What?'.

These twenty-six pairs of ganglia in the sympathetic nerve system, therefore, are divided into five groups which correspond to the five virtues represented by the pentagram: purity, justice, love, wisdom and truth. (See Figure 3, page 72).

Purity is linked to the four pairs of sacral ganglia at the base of the chain of ganglia, for purity is the base, the Foundation.

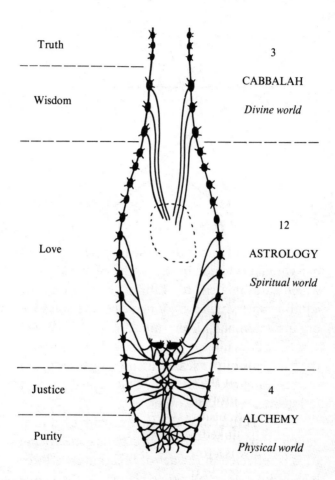

Truth

Wisdom

Love

Justice

Purity

3

CABBALAH

Divine world

12

ASTROLOGY

Spiritual world

4

ALCHEMY

Physical world

Figure 2. The chain of ganglia
and their corresponding virtues and numbers.

Figure 3. The pentagram

Justice corresponds to the four pairs of lumbar ganglia (located in the region of the kidneys which are related to Libra, the symbol of equilibrium) which are connected to the digestive organs (stomach, liver, intestines, etc). When someone does not eat wisely, the balance is upset, the two pans of the scales are no longer level and the resulting problems show that justice has had to intervene to restore order.

Love is linked to the twelve pairs of dorsal ganglia. Love is a force which expands one's being (this is reflected in the act of breathing); a force which links us to all other beings, to the whole universe, symbolized and represented by the twelve Constellations of the Zodiac.

Wisdom is connected to the three pairs of cervical ganglia which are linked to the heart by means of the cardiac nerves: true wisdom comes from the heart.

Truth is linked to the three pairs of cranial ganglia, for truth is the *summum,* the goal of all our endeavours. Truth is above everything else.

Truth, wisdom, love, justice and purity are our points of contact with the harmonious forces of the universe from which we receive so many blessings. Each one of these virtues enhances the functioning of the ganglia or organs to which it is linked, just as each and every fault against these virtues upsets that functioning.

For a very long time it was believed that there was no direct connection between the brain and the sympathetic nerve system, but we now know better. Science now recognizes that there is a very close link between the two. As the brain cannot act directly on the internal organs, it uses a conductor, the sympathetic system, and the solar plexus is the principal centre of this system. Initiates endeavour to raise this link between the solar plexus and the brain to the level of consciousness, for once it has become a conscious collaboration the rest is easy: by means of the solar plexus they can communicate with their physical organs and control and fortify them.

Our psychic condition is very closely connected to our physical condition. Sorrow, for example, acts on the sympathetic system and triggers the vasoconstrictor function, causing the walls of the arteries to contract. This contraction caused by sorrow reduces the flow of blood and, consequently, affects the digestion, respiration and so on, and then one feels pressured, ill-used and neglected. The feeling may not correspond to reality at all, but it is the impression one has! If, by contrast, we want to trigger reactions which expand and relax, we must call on joy and love. Instead of waking up every morning feeling depressed and thinking, 'I haven't any money. The woman I love is unfaithful to me. I still haven't got that letter I've been waiting for, etc., etc', you must do your utmost to cultivate positive, happy thoughts. A true disciple gets up every morning with the thought, 'Lord God, Creator of Heaven and Earth, thank you! I'm alive and well, I can breathe, walk about, sing, see and hear — You have given me all these priceless gifts. Thank you, thank you, thank you!' We should get up in the morning joyfully, with a heart full of gratitude to the Lord. If human beings grow old so quickly it is because they don't know how to call on joy to be their constant companion.

The solar plexus is an extremely important centre, and we must be careful to avoid whatever makes it tense because this, in turn, leads to the contraction of the blood vessels and other ducts and canals of the body. And if the blood and other body fluids can't circulate fast enough, waste products build up on the walls of the ducts and can lead to serious health problems. The thing which most seriously upsets the solar plexus is the chaotic, tempestuous manifestation of disorder in the astral body: fear, anger, jealousy and sexual passion. And as the solar plexus is the reservoir of our life forces, this loss of harmony deprives us of our magnetic energies. When you receive a severe shock or a sudden fright, you can feel that all the strength has gone out of you; your legs give way beneath you, your hands tremble and your head feels completely empty. This is a sign that your solar plexus has been drained of its energy.

So, as you see, it is possible to empty the solar plexus of its forces but it is also possible to replenish these forces, and it is this that a disciple must learn: how to replenish his solar plexus. Let me give you a few methods.

A tree is a storehouse of energies gathered both from the sun and from the earth, and man can draw on those energies. Choose a tall, sturdy tree, stand with your back to it, your left hand behind you with the palm touching the trunk of the tree and, at the same time, place the palm of your right hand on your solar plexus. Then concentrate mentally on the tree; talk to it, ask it to share some of its energy and strength with you. You will receive these energies with your left hand and pour them into your solar plexus with your right hand. It is a kind of 'energy transfusion.'

You can also strengthen your solar plexus by watching and listening to running water, a fountain, a spring or a waterfall. These methods are so simple that they seem insignificant, but you can get considerable benefit from them. Running water affects the solar plexus and gives it renewed vigour and it can then more effectively get rid of harmful elements. Very often we stare at a stream of running water unconsciously, without realizing how useful it could be for our spiritual life if we used it to advantage. In any case, we know so little about how to use all the elements nature supplies us with so generously!

An extremely simple method, if you're at home, is to lie down on your bed, place both hands on your solar plexus and imagine that you are drawing energy from the whole cosmos.

Another method is to plunge your hands into water or, better still, to do so with your feet: when you feel demagnetized, anxious or tense, prepare a basin of hot water and soak your feet in it consciously, then wash them carefully and with attention. This is an excellent way to influence your solar plexus and replenish its supply of energy, and you will find that your state of mind will improve immediately. In fact, if you find yourself unable to meditate one day, have a foot bath and you'll see that it will be much easier to concentrate!

There are ways, too, of communicating directly with one's solar plexus and getting it to give orders for the solution of certain problems. This is something that will be studied in the future. For the moment, however, it is not really possible to communicate with one's solar plexus; it has its own independent way of life and there is not much man can do about it. The most he can do is to influence it indirectly until such time as he can do so directly. And how can he influence it indirectly? Well, the very best way is to live a pure, sensible, luminous life. His way of life will affect his plexus and make it freer, releasing it from all the constraints that hamper it. And when the solar plexus is given a free hand it is capable of putting everything to rights in no time at all, for it is extremely powerful.

One meets so many people who are obviously overburdened, discouraged and worn out. Their problem is that they don't know how to work with their solar plexus; you can see this from the lack of light in their faces. A bleak, gloomy face without a glimmer of light in it is a

sure sign that the person's solar plexus is not functioning as it should. You, at least, who are listening to me, try to apply the methods I have given
you and work with your solar plexus, otherwise it
may be years before you are aware that it is there,
vibrant and wakeful within you, before you feel
it warming and relaxing you. If you don't
develop your solar plexus everything will be
centred in your brain, and however diligently
you watch the sunrise or meditate or do various
exercises, you will not get any good from them.
None of these things will really do you any good
until your solar plexus starts to show signs of life,
and you begin to feel that your consciousness has
at last reached even to your bowels. I could
describe that feeling to you, but what use would it
be? You wouldn't understand what I was saying
because to understand you have to experience it
for yourself. The intellect cannot give you any
idea of it. It's like toothache or falling in love: if
you have never experienced either one, no amount
of explanation will ever make you understand!
You can't understand until you have lived through
the experience, so there's no point in my trying
to explain. You have to work, work to change
your life and live harmoniously. That is the only
way to arouse your subtle centres to activity,
because they know only one law: the law of
harmony.

Unfortunately, what men feel and experience in life is rarely in tune with the harmony that reigns in the universe. And this is very grave, for when man opposes the laws and the forces and currents of the cosmos he is cutting himself off, hiding behind an impenetrable barrier of his own making between himself and the universe. Then the nourishing, life-giving forces flowing through the whole cosmos for the benefit of all creatures can no longer reach him to wash away his impurities and restore order, with the result that his health deteriorates. Yes, illness is simply the disorder that results when man severs his bonds with the cosmos and no longer maintains the vital relationship of mutual exchange.

Man is obliged to maintain a ceaseless current of exchange with the universe simply in order to stay alive: to eat, drink, breathe, absorb light and heat from the sun and receive the influence of cosmic rays. He cannot survive a single minute if this flow of exchange is interrupted, but he is so unconscious that he doesn't even realize that his life depends on this exchange. He spends his time cutting his ties with the universe and making it impossible for the cosmic forces to circulate in him, thus destroying the harmony which should normally mark the relationship between himself and the universe. And yet this harmony is the only thing that makes it possible for him to live with intensity and to fulfil himself creatively.

For this reason you must acquire the habit of devoting a few minutes every day to restoring harmony between yourself and the cosmos and trying to vibrate in rhythm with every creature in existence. Say, 'I sincerely want to live in harmony with you. I love you, I love you. All blessings on you..' This exercise sets the energies circulating again. Even the wisest and holiest of men sometimes experience moments in which they are troubled and out of tune with the universe, but because they are wise they are aware of it. They realize at once that their vibrations have changed and they immediately take steps to restore harmony. Whereas most people remain in a state of disharmony for days and weeks and even years until, in the end, they simply fade away.

Once and for all, then, make up your minds to understand the laws of nature, to learn how man is built and what kind of relationship he must have with these laws. If you are concerned about your own happiness and fulfilment you must pay attention to the question of harmony and take steps to be in harmony with the whole universe. Obviously, you will not achieve this perfectly all at once, but if you persevere the day will come when you feel that your whole being, from head to foot, is in communion and vibrating in harmony with the life of the cosmos!

A child in the womb is attached to its mother and receives nourishment from her by means of the umbilical cord, situated in the area of the solar plexus. At birth this bond between the child and its mother is cut and one might suppose, therefore, that birth is the passage from a state of dependency to one of independence. In fact, though, even after birth, man is not completely independent. His solar plexus is linked by another, etheric umbilical cord to Mother Nature who bears him in her womb and nourishes and sustains him. This is why certain schools of spirituality in the East teach their disciples to concentrate on their navel. Of course, Westerners, who see only the outer aspect of things, jeer at 'fools who spend their lives contemplating their belly-button', but it is they who are the fools. They have simply missed the point: those who meditate on their navel in order to affirm and renew their ties with the cosmos, experience a deep sense of fulfilment. Aware of the fact that they are still dependent on Mother Nature, they concentrate on cleansing and purifying this channel through which she sends them all those precious elements they need.

To the extent to which men maintain this bond with nature, it would be true to say that the vast majority are still unborn: they have not cut the umbilical cord. In order to be born they will have to leave the womb in which they are still sleeping. A man is born for the first time when he is brought into the world by his physical mother, but his true birth, that which is known in an Initiatic context as the Second Birth, can only happen when he severs his attachment to what the philosophers call 'natural Nature' and enters the realm of divine nature. Only then will he be born to true consciousness and enlightenment.

II

It is often said that the heart is the organ that understands, that discernment is a faculty of the heart. Even the Gospels speak of the heart that understands. But what heart are they talking about? Not the physical heart, obviously, the organ which pumps blood through the body. No, the true heart of man, the Initiatic heart, is the solar plexus. It is the solar plexus which senses, grasps and comprehends the great truths of the cosmos. The brain can only study a little, write and talk and, above all, show off, even if it has no very clear idea of what it is talking about! If you look around you today, you will see a great deal of writing and discussing going on, but no real understanding, for the brain is incapable of true comprehension. Things have to be experienced in order to be understood, experienced with every fibre of one's being.

When you feel an emotion, terror, anguish or love, you don't feel it in your brain or even in your physical heart; you feel it in your solar plexus. When the Initiates said that man's true heart was in the solar plexus, therefore, it showed that their knowledge of human anatomy and physiology was far more complete and accurate than that of the modern biologist who only sees the material, physical aspects. This is a denial of the true reality of human beings. Initiates, on the contrary, are concerned, first and foremost, with the subtle, invisible dimension. Their knowledge is prodigious but they keep many things secret because it would be too dangerous to publish them to the world at large; they reveal them to only a few and the others have to discover them for themselves.

You must realize that the solar plexus controls the majority of the functions of the physical body and, above all, that it is the solar plexus which created and which continues to nourish the brain. Yes, the brain is the creation, the offspring of the solar plexus. This is why the solar plexus feeds the brain and keeps it supplied with everything it needs. If it ceases to do so a person becomes incapable of activity, he has a headache or feels drowsy and cannot think any more.

The brain is not cut off from the solar plexus, but it has not yet learned how to communicate with it, and this is why it cannot always take advantage of the support provided by the solar plexus. As I have already explained, the solar plexus is a brain, but a brain in reverse, for in the brain the grey matter is on the outside and the white matter on the inside, whereas in the solar plexus it is the opposite. The grey matter which is composed of nerve cells makes it possible to think, while the white matter, composed of nerve fibres, makes it possible to feel. Thanks to its outer layer of white matter, therefore, the solar plexus can feel everything that goes on in the body, in every single cell, and is therefore able constantly to restore order and balance. The brain feels nothing at all until things have reached very serious proportions, and even then it doesn't know what to do about it. If your heart is beating too fast or too slowly, or if you have a stomachache, the brain can do nothing about it and, what is more, that is not its job! But if you make sure that the solar plexus has the conditions it needs to function correctly, it can soon put everything right. You couldn't begin to imagine what an extraordinary pharmacopoeia it possesses and, as it is in touch with all the organs of your body and with each and every cell, it can intervene where necessary. It is far better equipped, therefore, than the brain.

But this has never been properly explained, even by medical science.

With the development of the brain man attained the self-awareness which enabled him to become an individual. The solar plexus, by contrast, being the seat of the subconscious, maintains man's contact with the ocean of universal life, with the whole cosmos, and this is something the brain cannot do — at least, not yet. One day this communication will be possible, but the brain was formed too recently and is still insufficiently developed, whereas the solar plexus has existed far longer. The brain developed relatively recently in animals and even more recently in men. In fact an ant's brain, for instance, is far more perfectly organized than a man's, because ants are older than men! The human brain is still not fully organized, but this will come, for its mission is to record the totality of knowledge and to give birth to notions still beyond our ken. But, I repeat, the one in charge at the moment, the one who controls and commands all the others, is the solar plexus in conjunction with the Hara centre, situated a little lower down.

Modern man is engaged in his own destruction because the greater part of his activities are cerebral: study, calculations, worries, and so on. And as the brain is not designed to stand up to so much strain, much of the nervous ill-health so prevalent today stems from the fact that the brain is overloaded. You must learn, therefore, to divide the burden between the two centres: the solar plexus, in the belly, and the brain in the head. This is the only way to be balanced. It is a law of mechanics: if you want to balance a pair of scales you have to put something in both pans, not only on one side.

The brain is only an instrument, it is not an independent organism, and any instrument has to be properly looked after if it is to work properly. Take the example of a motor or an electric torch: if you reduce or cut off the power supply it will work less efficiently. The human brain is like a torch which can be switched on and which can see reality and reason about it. Yes, but the trouble is that, in most people, the torch is not very efficient, it is often no more than a candle, and it doesn't give out much light. So it has to be plugged in to an inexhaustible source of energy which will allow it to develop its full potential; and that source is the solar plexus. Why did the ancients call it the 'solar' plexus? Because it is linked to the sun, and the sun is the heart of our planetary system.

What is the relationship between the solar plexus and the brain? They are the two poles: the one masculine and emissive and the other, feminine and receptive. You can find this polarity reflected in every sphere of nature. Take the case of a married couple: the husband spends almost all his time working so as to earn money to buy clothes, jewelry and perfumes for his wife. She is elegant, expensively dressed and enormously attractive, while he, poor devil, slaves away for her sake in his dirty old working clothes. Of course, it could be just the other way round, but I am speaking symbolically.

The solar plexus and the brain are so intimately connected that either can help or hinder the other. God has not given powers and possibilities to only one of them, just as, in the case of men and women, God has not given all power to man and none to woman. No, He has given powers to both, but so different that they can only be made fully manifest when the two principles are united and work together towards a single goal. Woman cannot bring to the partnership the gifts that man brings, nor can man bring the same gifts as woman, but when they combine their powers the results are fantastic. And in this question of the two 'brains', the solar plexus and the brain in the head, it is important to understand how they are polarized as masculine and feminine, how they interact and influence each other and the power they have over matter.

The Solar Plexus

You know the experiment of the Crookᵢ tube (see below): when an electric current ᵢ applied between two electrodes in the tube, the cathode emits a flow of electrons in the direction of the anode. The cathode remains dark but the anode lights up.

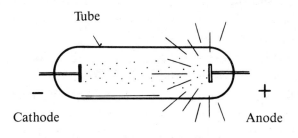

Figure 4. Crooke's Tube

This experiment is an excellent illustration of the relationship between the masculine and the feminine principles. Everywhere, throughout the whole of nature, you can see these two principles at work. It is this Initiatic Science which Melchizedek revealed to Abraham: the existence of the two principles which manifest themselves in a multitude of different forms throughout the universe, and the manner in which they work together.

The brain manifests itself in all kinds of ways: it speaks, gives orders, organizes things, shouts and gesticulates and generally makes a fuss. But where does it get the power to do all that? It is the solar plexus that supplies the brain with energy, but without calling attention to itself in any way. The solar plexus is always there, but behind the scenes; so quiet and discreet that no one ever suspects its presence. It is like the humble, hard-working husband! Although, in point of fact it plays the feminine role: the mother that feeds her young, the infinite wealth and inexhaustible reservoirs of nature. And the brain? Well, since it was formed by the solar plexus, the brain is its child. Or, if you prefer, the brain is the husband who is always holding forth, arguing, issuing anathemas in all directions, while his wife quietly gets on with her humble tasks in the background. You have to understand these changes of polarity.

The brain is active and dynamic but it tires very quickly if the solar plexus doesn't subsidize it regularly. For this reason, before undertaking any major intellectual task, a disciple should first prepare the solar plexus. The brain is capable of great things, but on condition that the solar plexus keeps it supplied with energy. The source, therefore, the projector, is the solar plexus and the brain is the screen which manifests, expresses and publishes whatever the plexus feeds to it. The pictures projected onto the screen of the brain come from the plexus. Whether good or bad, they are all produced on the screen, just as at the cinema. The only difference is that, at the cinema, the masculine principle is the cameraman or his projector which projects the images onto the screen, and the screen represents the feminine principle, the matter onto which the spirit projects forces and energies. As you see: yet another change of polarity!

When you want to meditate or to undertake any intense intellectual activity, don't rush into it or try to concentrate suddenly, without preparation, otherwise your brain will just seize up and you won't accomplish anything worthwhile. Begin by concentrating on your solar plexus and then, when you feel that you have reached a state of peace and inner warmth, you can begin to work because your brain will be sustained and nourished by the energies flowing from your plexus. And if, while you are working, you feel that your brain is beginning to flag, massage your solar plexus with a circular motion, anti-clockwise. In a very few minutes you will feel that your thought is once more flowing freely and you can get back to work.

You have to learn to share out the work between the brain and the solar plexus just as in a marriage, in which the husband and wife live in harmony and share the work. In these conditions the brain will be capable of manifesting all the powers stored in the plexus. The solar plexus has archives in which all the knowledge it has ever acquired since the most remote past is stored, and it is up to the brain to retrieve this knowledge and to express it. The brain is simply an instrument designed to bring to light all the treasures buried in the depths of our beings.

As we have seen, the solar plexus is also a brain, but reversed. The white matter, which is on the outside of the solar plexus, is in touch with the white matter on the inside of the brain, and the grey matter which is on the inside of the plexus, is in touch with the grey matter on the outside of the brain. Here is yet another reversal of position, a crossing over, and it takes place at the level of the neck. For this reason, if you feel that communications are not getting through as they should, you can massage your neck in the region of the cervical vertebrae, and this will get the currents flowing again between the solar plexus and the brain. The neck is an extremely important passageway; if you grip someone's neck too violently you can kill him, because the life flowing from the solar plexus can no longer reach the brain. This gives you some idea of how important these nerve centres are, but medical science has not yet studied the question of the crossing over that occurs in the neck (the right hemisphere of the brain which controls the left side of the body and vice versa) from the point of view of the cosmic correspondences.

When you have learned to concentrate on the solar plexus with a deeply loving attitude you will be able to tap its immense resources of energy and direct them to the brain. And since the brain is a screen on which images can be projected, the more perfectly the plexus projects its images, the more energetic and capable of action one becomes.

We see here, once again, a phenomenon which is present in every sphere of life. I have already spoken to you, a long time ago, about the 'dark sun' from which our own sun receives its energy. This dark sun, which never stops giving, is the masculine principle, and our sun represents the feminine principle in relation to it, for it receives from it the energy which enables it to shine. I am not saying that I have actually seen the dark sun, but I have seen it inwardly : it is a reality, and without it there would be no sun to shine in the heavens. Here again we have Crooke's Tube, the cathode and the anode, but on the scale of the whole universe.

How clear and simple all this is ! Everywhere, in every dimension of the universe, these two principles are at work. Let me give you yet another example: that of a tree. A tree consists of roots, a trunk and branches. The roots supply the energy that makes it possible for leaves, flowers and fruit to appear on the branches. The roots are hidden, invisible, but if you get rid of them, the visible parts of the tree will wither and die. That which is visible is always the consequence of something which is invisible, buried deep under the surface. In man the solar plexus represents the roots, and his trunk and limbs represent the trunk and branches of the tree. Man is like a tree, with roots, a trunk, branches and, in the brain, flowers and fruit. The solar plexus is the most important part of man because it is the root; the root is always the most important: if anything goes wrong with the roots, the whole plant deteriorates. So, you see, this is just one more argument which no one can contest: if you destroy the roots the tree will die.

When you want to meditate you choose a spiritual subject on which to concentrate and then you can watch your thoughts unfold, as it were, as they follow the contours of the subject. It is almost as though you could see their shapes and colours: this is an activity of the brain. But when your meditation takes you onto a higher plane, you feel that your brain ceases to be actively in charge and the solar plexus takes over. You no longer grasp things analytically, with the intellect; instead, you have a synthetic grasp of reality and you begin to vibrate in harmony with the subject of your meditation, to enjoy a marvellous sense of fulfilment: your meditation becomes contemplation. Your thought, your mental activity, has become contemplation of things so shining and wondrous that your vibrations become more and more intense. Without realizing just how it can be so, you know with absolute certainty that you understand things far better than when you use your intellect. Yes, and this is simply because you have touched the heart of the universe.

When you study, ponder and understand things intellectually it does not mean that you have touched the heart of the universe: no, this activity of the brain is no more than a first approach. You can only touch the heart of the universe with your own heart. When your heart — your solar plexus — begins to feel and love and vibrate with great intensity, then, yes! You can then touch and move the heart of the universe, the heart of God Himself, and the life-giving, illuminating currents, forces and energies of that heart will flood into you. When a powerful stream of love pours out from your heart, the law of affinity, the law of echo reflection, triggers a response from the heart of the universe. To touch the heart of the universe is to know, feel and enter into the plans and intentions of the Eternal One, the Soul of the Universe. And this is something that you will never attain by means of knowledge, book-learning or lectures, however eloquent they may be.

In order to touch the heart of the universe you have to vibrate on the same wavelength, that is, to emanate the same disinterested love. When all your wishes and desires and everything you pray for no longer concern only your own interests but the good of humanity and the universe as a whole, then your heart vibrates in rhythm with the heart of the universe; it is tuned to the same wavelength. And since the heart of the universe is the source of all happiness and all loveliness, the source of all poetry and music, of all that is splendid and divine, then you will receive that life, that happiness and all that splendour! Then you will taste fulfilment.

When you touch someone's heart he is ready to give you everything you ask for; he opens his doors to you and gives you all he has. There are days when you make speeches to the powerful entities on high in an attempt to impress them or move them to pity, but your efforts are in vain. They slam the door in your face, saying, 'We don't know what you're talking about!' On other days you need say nothing at all; you just look, and they welcome you: 'Come in! Come in! Here, you can have this... Take that too: it's yours!' Can you explain this? You will have to find the secret.

I remember that I spoke to you, one day, about the old-fashioned crystal sets. Some fifty or sixty years ago, when radios where less efficient and far less widespread than they are today, people used to make their own crystal sets. In order to receive radio waves you had to move a very fine needle over the surface of a galenoid crystal until you made contact. As soon as the needle reached a certain spot one heard music or voices, while on other spots nothing came through. This phenomenon gave me matter for much reflection! You can slide your little needle back and forth across the crystal and hear nothing — and yet the needle is in contact with the surface. Yes, but you're not touching its heart, for that crystal also has a heart! As soon as you touch the heart you can hear music. And in the universe, also, there is a heart, but we are ignorant of its laws so we can't make contact or get onto its wavelength to receive its signals and the revelations they hold.

In order to touch the heart of the universe you have to intensify your love. And this is something that has to be done with the solar plexus. As I have said, when you do this your mental activity ceases: you project a powerful beam of energy, a strong current of love, and although it is you who are in control, yet your brain remains at rest. You understand, you are conscious and you direct your energies, without tension or activity of the brain. How is this possible? The explanation is that there is another form of thought, another kind of comprehension, and this is what you need to discover.

4

THE HARA CENTRE

If you go to India one day it may surprise you to see that many saddhus and yogis are noticeably pot-bellied although they eat hardly anything! And you will probably have noticed that almost all the statues of Buddha or other sages portray them with a generous paunch. The reason for this is that, in an Initiate, a well-rounded paunch is a sign of power and strength, an indication of the spiritual reserves he has accumulated thanks to years of special breathing exercises. Prolonged breathing exercises develop this region of the body because it is there that certain elements which enable an Initiate to heal sickness and disintegrate harmful influences are stored. A pot-belly, therefore, can be the result either of a materialistic way of life or of a very spiritual way of life. If a man's face reveals that he is only interested in eating, drinking and sleeping then, of course, his corpulence is a bad sign; it indicates a coarse, materialistic, sensual person. But if he is pure, clairvoyant and intelligent, then his stoutness shows that he has substantial reserves which he can call upon to heal others and do a lot of good things which someone who is weedy and skinny could not do because, poor creature, he lacks the resources.

Look at the Japanese: some of them have an enormous paunch and yet they are very supple and strong and very intelligent. The explanation is that they develop what they call the Hara centre. This is the centre situated just four centimetres below the navel. In Japanese *hara* means belly and the expression *hara-kiri*, which we have all heard of, means to commit suicide by opening the belly. According to Japanese sages, the Hara is man's life-centre, his centre of gravity, the universal centre; and when one concentrates on it and develops it to the full, one becomes tireless and invincible. The most striking characteristic in those who have worked to develop their Hara centre is that they are extraordinarily well balanced.

A great many of the problems characteristic of our times come, as I have already told you, from the fact that people in the West have upset the balance of their lives. They are no longer centred as they should be, in their centre of gravity, their life-centre. Instead, the brain, which by rights is on the periphery of man, has usurped the central position. Too much thought, too many cares, too much cerebral activity have unbalanced man. This is why, when his system receives a shock of any kind he is so easily knocked off balance and is unable to recover: his centre of gravity which would normally remedy the situation is not functioning correctly. If he knew how to concentrate on the Hara centre and develop it correctly it wouldn't matter how much nervous energy he spent, he would never feel exhausted.

Of course, for Westerners, there is the problem that for a long time the force-centres situated lower down in the physical body were considered unworthy of any part in the spiritual life. Even I, for years, when I spoke of the 'centre', I almost always meant the Supreme Centre, God Himself, the First Cause. I never told you that, in his physical body, man's true centre was there, just below the navel. It has taken years to prepare you to accept this, but now you are ready to penetrate and explore this centre, to learn to develop it and, thereby, discover the source of your being. For it is there that you will find your source! What I did tell you, often and often, is that you must dig: 'Don't look for solutions outside yourself or on the surface. Dig, dig deep and you'll find gold and oil!' Of course this was symbolic. It was a way of saying that this is where you have to dig: in the subconscious.

The Hara centre is mentioned in many esoteric books, but often in very different ways. In fact some passages from ancient Christian authors show that they knew of this centre. In his book, 'The Twelve Keys', the famous alchemist, Basile Valentin, encourages adepts to descend into the earth's centre to seek the Philosopher's Stone. He says: *Visita interiora terrae; rectificando invenies occultum lapidem, veram medicinam*, which means: 'Visit the bowels of the Earth; if you rectify you will find the hidden Stone, the true medicine.' If you take the first letter of each of the Latin words: *Visita Interiora Terrae,* etc., you will find that they form the word VITRIOLUM. In fact, of course, Valentine was not talking about descending into the centre of the planet, but into our own centre, into our own physical bodies, for it is there that we shall find materials, treasures and wealth of every sort.

The three principal deities of the Hindu Pantheon are Brahma, Vishnu and Shiva, and Hindu sacred scriptures say that Brahma resides in the belly, Vishnu in the region of the heart and lungs and Shiva in the brain. Why should Brahma, the creator, be said to reside in the belly? If it is such a despicable region and the brain, on the contrary is so noble, one would have thought that Hindu mystics would have assigned Brahma to the brain. But no, it is Shiva who is associated with the brain, because Shiva is the great destroyer. Brahma is the creator; Vishnu is the preserver, he who repairs, sustains and nourishes, while Shiva is the destroyer. And if Shiva has been identified with the brain it is because the brain — that is to say the lower mental body — divides, dissects, analyses and disintegrates reality. It is the brain that divides men one from another and leads them into error.

Since it is in the belly that children are conceived and formed it is an extremely important part of the body: there is nothing shameful about it. Surely life would not choose a place of shame in which to be conceived! If Cosmic Intelligence has chosen this region, it must be because It considers it to be sacred. This being so, why should man despise it? Of course, it is true that it is not especially beautiful — at least, not according to our notion of beauty — but there must be a reason why life takes its origin there. Not only is the womb in which a mother carries her child, in the belly, but the child draws nourishment and strength into its own belly through its umbilical cord. The Russians have a term for this area which includes the solar plexus and Hara centre; it is *jivot,* and in Bulgarian *jivot* means 'life'. Yes, this is where life takes its source, and from here it radiates and spreads to the other organs. The brain, therefore, is also dependent on this centre and draws life from it. Once again we can refer to the comparison with a tree: the most important part of a tree is its roots, that part which is hidden under the ground, obscure and discreetly out of sight. Well, there you have it: the Hara centre and the solar plexus are our roots. And if we go down into our roots to see what nature has put there, we shall discover a world of the most extraordinary wealth and variety of materials and energies: a veritable mine, an inexhaustible source.

The belly is where life is created. Yes, the source of life is there, in the belly. Even the Gospels say, 'Out of his belly will flow rivers of living water.' Why the belly? Why not the brain or the lungs? What is so special about this region of the body that living waters should flow from it? It is because Brahma, the Father, the Creator abides here. But in order to feel this, in order to experience his presence and communicate with him it takes years and years of effort. He is there but we don't profit in any way from his presence because we are fully occupied with Shiva. Even in India there are very few temples dedicated to Brahma; more are dedicated to Vishnu and many more again to Shiva. Why is this? Is it from fear of Shiva, because he is the destroyer? Do men honour him in order to appease him and protect themselves? Whereas with Brahma there is no need to be afraid: he is the creator, there is no danger that he will ever harm us. Perhaps that is why he is neglected!

For years now I have been instructing you only in the things of the higher spheres: the world of consciousness and light. But in fact, this has been simply to prepare you to penetrate into the depths of your own being. For, if you want to know yourself as you truly are, you have to know both regions: that which is above as well as that which is below. That which is above are the brain centres, and that which is below are what the Japanese sages call the Hara.

The Hara represents the subconscious, the obscure depths of man. But of course these dark regions are very dangerous, and that is why it is important to begin by exploring the higher ground and only later, when one has become really stalwart, when one has acquired all the necessary arms and equipment, can one start to go down into the abyss to see what secrets it holds. All the wealth of the world lies underground: gold, precious stones and rare metals, coal and oil, they are all hidden under the soil, and a multitude of spirits and invisible entities works amongst them. And in the psychic world, just as in the physical world, everything is hidden down

below, not exposed for all to see above ground.
But Hell and its monsters are also down below,
and this is why, before going down, we have to
learn to protect ourselves, otherwise we shall simply be swallowed up. So now you understand why
our Teaching begins with the world above. We
have to arm ourselves with light before confront-
ing darkness.

Man is no more capable of being in touch
with his Hara centre than he is of contacting his
solar plexus, because he doesn't have direct access
to his own subconscious, he can only reach it by
indirect means, that is by the way he lives. If the
Hara centre is not harmoniously aligned with the
universe, therefore, it is because his way of life is
orderless, chaotic and irrational, and makes it
impossible for him to receive the fragrance
emanating from the Universal Soul.

Now, I will give you an exercise you can do
with the Hara centre during your meditation. If
you do it in a spirit of purity, abnegation and
complete disinterestedness, it can help you to
become stronger and regain your balance: it consists simply in concentrating on the Hara centre
while you place both hands on it. But, as I say,
you must do this in a spirit of purity and for the
good of all mankind, otherwise you can easily
awaken other centres in that area and find yourself dragged down into the murky depths of your

lower self. Before attempting to work with the Hara, therefore, you have to prepare yourselves. When you are ready, you can explore these depths without danger, for this is the abyss, the veritable underworld of human nature.

Of course, psychoanalysts have explored some areas of the subconscious, but they are still a very long way from understanding the mysteries of the Hara centre and how this centre buried in the depths of the subconscious is linked with the superconsciousness. When an Initiate speaks of joining the head and tail of the serpent he is saying that we must join the lower centres or Chakras to Sahasrara, the crown Chakra situated in the brain. But how can you hope to accomplish anything worthwhile in these perilous lower regions if you have not, first of all, worked at more accessible things? You must begin by purifying and strengthening yourself and later, when you feel ready to do so, you can venture into the lower regions: this is an experience that lies ahead of you, and you must prepare for it.

Alchemists speak of the 'light which is born of darkness'. Darkness is infinitely vaster than light: it embraces and penetrates all things, whereas light is like a tiny spark wrapped in darkness. Darkness is the root of all being. Every phenomenon visible on earth, all manifestations and materialisations spring from darkness; like children in the womb of Mother Nature, all energies and elements are attached to her by a kind of umbilical cord through which they draw sustenance from the Cosmic Soul.

'The light which is born of darkness'! Doesn't this speak to us of the profound symbolism of the Christmas Crib, the dark stable in which Jesus was born? Why did Jesus have to be born in a manger, between an ox and an ass, rather than in a palace or temple or a large, sumptuously appointed house? Because, just as a physical baby is born from the lower part of the body, when a spiritual child is born, when the Christ is born in man, He too is born from the lower region, the Hara centre. The Hara is the crib, and the ox and ass are the liver and spleen on either side. And Angels sing and rejoice in the heavens, because this birth, the Second Birth, is a joyful event in which all Heaven takes part.

The events which surrounded the birth of Jesus occur again each time a human being has become capable of being born again. The ass is there as well as the ox, the Magi, the Angels, the Virgin and the Child in the manger. This is not something which happened only once, two thousand years ago in Palestine; it is constantly being re-enacted. And if we want this Child to be born in us we must know how to attract it and how to nurture and cherish it within ourselves.

The birth of Jesus in a manger, therefore, is an initiatic symbol of the deepest significance. It is here, in the Hara Chakra, in this crib flanked on either side by the ox and the ass — the liver and the spleen — that a disciple has to bring to birth the divine infant, the child Jesus, a new consciousness.*

Hermes Trismegistus said, 'That which is below is like to that which is above, and that which is above is like to that which is below.' It is not, as many have thought, a question of things below being identical, exact replicas of things above. That which is below is certainly not identical with that which is above. That which is below is like that which is above in the sense that the laws and functions are the same. To say that something is 'like' another does not mean that they are exactly the same. When you see a house reflected in water, that which is above, in the real world, is like that which is below in the reflected world, but the two worlds are not identical.

There are, therefore, two worlds: the world of reflection and illusion below, and the world of

* See 'Christmas' in *Christmas and Easter in the Initiatic Tradition*, (Collection Izvor No 209).

reality above. In each of the two worlds there is also an 'above' and a 'below', so that that which is below in the world of illusion corresponds to that which is above in the world of reality. And since the Creator is on the highest plane of the divine hierarchy, in man, who is a reflection of that hierarchy, the creative function is at the lowest level. I have already spoken to you a long time ago about this reversal when I told you that stones, minerals and crystals are the reflection below of the divine world, above. The lower centres in man correspond to the highest levels in the Divine world, for in man, the microcosm, the macrocosm finds its reflection upside down! This is why Brahma, the Creator, is said to dwell in man's belly.

The subject is infinitely vast but I have already said a great deal — enough for the moment, at any rate. If I told you more you wouldn't know what to do with it; it would only burden you. Of course, I know, everyone always wants to know everything, but that is simply curiosity! In true Initiatic Teaching what matters is that the disciples put things into practice and learn to rely on their own forces, their own capabilities, in order to accomplish something valid. I am well aware that you won't like it when I say that, because you are accustomed to looking for solutions outside yourselves. And it is precisely for that reason that the force-centres within you don't function as they were intended to: they are rusty and the currents cannot flow as they should. Of course, there are a few mystics, philosophers and spiritual people who are accustomed to working with their inner resources, but the great majority of human beings are cripples in this respect: they have neither the strength nor the will to undertake this work on themselves.

Perhaps you will say that you do work on yourselves but that you don't get any results. Of course, none of this is easy and the question of reincarnation comes into it too. If this is the first incarnation in which you have tried to work with these centres you need not be surprised if you are finding it difficult: they have been left idle and immobile for centuries, so you can hardly expect anything else. But for those who have already done some work in this line in previous incarnations, and who continue to do so in their present life, then, naturally, they will find it less difficult and will get some results.

So this is why I am telling you to hurry up and start to do something about it in this incarnation, knowing that if you don't begin now, you will not be able to do so next time, either. For the moment you may obtain only very meagre results, but that doesn't matter; at least you will have begun. In your next incarnation you will go on from there, and then you will get substantial results. So the important thing is that now, in this incarnation, you begin to release the divine currents within.

5

KUNDALINI FORCE

The Book of Revelation ends with St. John's vision of the heavenly city, the New Jerusalem, and a description of the walls, the foundations and the twelve gates. Through that city flows a great river:

'And he showed me a pure river of water of life, clear as crystal, proceeding from the throne of God and of the Lamb. In the middle of its street, and on either side of the river, was the tree of life, which bore twelve fruits, each tree yielding its fruit every month. And the leaves of the tree were for the healing of the nations.'

How can the tree be on both sides of the river? If you take this description literally it doesn't make sense. In reality, of course, the tree astride the river is a symbol; it exists also in us, and the river, too, flows through us. For it is we who are the city, and in the centre of that city — that is in the solar plexus — flows a river with a tree growing on its banks. The solar plexus represents both the tree growing on either side of the river and the river itself, the currents and vital forces flowing through it. And where are the roots of this tree? The roots are the twelve pairs of dorsal ganglia and nerves: twelve branches which produce twelve fruits a year and they, in turn, are linked to the twelve signs of the Zodiac.

Let us look, now, at the particular properties of these twelve fruits. The first, Aries, makes a person active, dynamic and purposeful. The second, Taurus, gives great sensitivity and a kind, affectionate nature. The third fruit, Gemini, incites to study, travel and a wide diversity of interests. The fourth, Cancer, gives possibilities for mediumship and the perception of invisible currents and subtle beings. The fifth fruit, Leo, confers magnanimity and the courage needed to help and save others. The sixth, Virgo, purifies and cleanses. The seventh, Libra, gives the possibility of taking up the Divine Cause and restoring cosmic balance within oneself. The eighth fruit, Scorpio, throws light on death and the after-life. The ninth, Sagittarius, bestows a taste for philosophical and religious subjects. The tenth, Capricorn, inspires power and authority in dealing both with oneself and with others. The eleventh fruit, Aquarius, gives a sense of universality and international brotherhood, and the

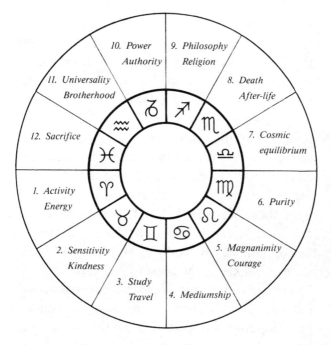

Figure 5. The Twelve Signs of the Zodiac
and their Qualities

twelfth, Pisces, gives a spirit of sacrifice and the ability not only to put up with suffering, but to recognize and rejoice in the benefits to be gained from it.

So there you have the attributes of the twelve fruits of the Tree of Life which, of course, is none other than the Sephirotic Tree described in the Cabbalah, with the ten Sephiroth: Kether, Chokmah, Binah, Chesed, Geburah, Tiphareth, Netzach, Hod, Yesod and Malkuth. Kether is the seed which contains the potential of the whole Tree; Chokmah is the nucleus which splits into two, allowing the shoot, Binah, to emerge; Chesed is the trunk; Geburah, branches; Tiphareth, the buds; Netzach, the leaves; Hod, the flowers, Yesod, the fruit, and Malkuth, the seed which is buried in the soil and which produces another tree. Here, again, we have a manifestation of the axiom, 'That which is below is like to that which is above', and you can understand why Jesus compared the Kingdom of God (Malkuth) to a tiny mustard seed which grows into a mighty tree in which all the birds of the air come to seek shelter.

St. John said that 'the leaves of the tree were for the healing of the nations'. So it is not only the fruits of the tree which accomplish miracles, but also the leaves and even the roots.

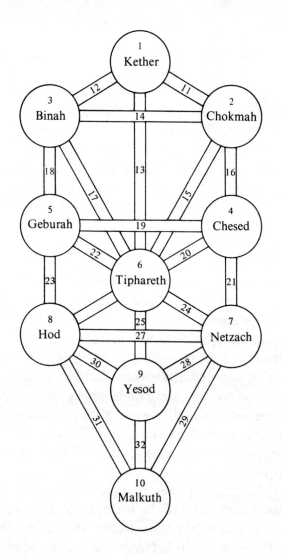

Figure 6. The Sephirotic Tree

The roots of the Tree of Life which St.John describes as being on both banks of the river, therefore, are the groups of nerves and ganglia on either side of the spine. The spinal column is the link between heaven and earth — our heaven and our earth. The river, says St. John, takes its source at the top of the mountain, 'proceeding from the throne of God'. In man, the top of the mountain, heaven, is his head, and the earth his belly. Under the earth burns a great fire which, from time to time, produces violent volcanic eruptions. This subterranean fire nests at the base of the spinal cord; it is the subterranean power of Kundalini, and it is closely associated both with the stomach and the sexual organs. For the moment, man's spine has a purely anatomical, physiological function; its spiritual potential is still dormant. So far, only Initiates have succeeded, thanks to the powers of Kundalini which they have awakened, in mobilising the spiritual potential of the spinal cord and in using it to accomplish tremendous spiritual and magical work in the world.

Kundalini power is coiled like a serpent asleep at the base of the spinal cord. This is the power which has been called Mother of the Universe, and which Hermes Trismegistus calls the 'strong fortitude of all strength'. Once awakened it may flow either up or down. If it moves upwards it is very beneficial and favours great spiritual development, but if, on the contrary, it rushes downwards it can have disastrous results. He who awakens the power of Kundalini without being absolutely pure and wholly in control of himself becomes a prey to uncontrollable sexual passions which plunge him at lightning speed into the deepest abyss, and to inordinate, overweening ambition which leads him to defy the whole world. This is why disciples are strongly advised not to attempt to arouse the Kundalini force before they have cultivated great purity and humility, for this most powerful of all forces, is just as liable to destroy as to create. In point of fact Kundalini can be aroused on different levels : she can be aroused seven times, for she sleeps with seven sleeps and is hidden by seven veils of matter.

In one way it is quite easy to awaken Kundalini, but what is important, indeed essential, is to know what orientation to give to her energies and how to guide them, and this is much more difficult. The forces of Kundalini are not subject to man's will and cannot be driven in whatever direction he chooses ; they will follow the direction determined by his qualities and virtues. When the Fiery Serpent awakes it rushes headlong towards the nearest source of nourishment, and if this happens to be in a man's lower nature, then that is where the Serpent goes, and the man is doomed and dragged down into the Pit. Whereas, if he can offer the Serpent nourishment on a higher plane, then it will rise into the higher levels of his being.

When Kundalini rises she passes through the channel called Sushumna in the spinal cord. On either side of Sushumna are two other channels: Ida, which is negatively polarized and linked to the Moon, and Pingala, positively polarized and linked to the Sun. These two channels interweave upwards in a spiral movement, until Ida terminates in the left nostril and Pingala in the right. This is why breathing exercises are considered most effective in awakening the Kundalini force.

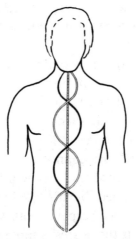

Figure 7.   Pingala (white) and Ida (black)
spiralling upwards around Sushumna

When you block up the right nostril and breathe through the left one, you produce a current which flows via the channel Ida, and reaches Muladhara, the centre in which Kundalini lies asleep. As it passes through Muladhara it produces a very, very slight vibration which contributes to rousing Kundalini just a little. Similarly, when you block up the left nostril, and breathe through the right one, the current flows via the channel of Pingala, and it too causes the Muladhara Chakra to vibrate very, very slightly, giving the Kundalini force yet another tiny impulse, and so on. By doing these breathing exercises every morning, therefore, gently, little by little, you awaken the Kundalini force, but you must be careful not to prolong these exercises unduly.

When I was in India I heard about all the different methods yogis used to arouse the Kundalini force. Some of them are almost unbelievable: one, for instance consists in introducing a tiny silver thread into a spot that shall remain unnamed! It is amazing what insane things some people are ready to do to awaken this force!

The best advice for Westerners, though, is not to attempt to awaken this force, but to live a life of purity in conformity with the divine laws. Kundalini will awake of her own accord when the time is right: it is very important not to rush things. Every other approach is dangerous, for this force is like a raging fire which can tear and even destroy certain of your physical organs. But when everything takes its natural course, gently and without shocks of any kind, then man awakens harmoniously to a consciousness of the divine world.

I can sense your tremendous desire to make whatever effort has to be made to reach this level of awareness. Yes, you may begin at once, but you must be very cautious and reasonable and not launch yourselves into it without guidance, otherwise you may well lose your balance and even destroy yourselves. So don't be in a hurry: it will come, gradually and gently. All the different exercises we do here, are forms of yoga which will make it possible, one day, for you to awaken the Kundalini force. A lot of people think that you have to go to India to find real spirituality. Certainly, it is excellent to go to India, but you must also realize that the Teaching of the Universal White Brotherhood is the true Teaching of Christ and that it provides a modern form of yoga perfectly adapted to Western mentalities.

Indian sages say that before freeing the Kundalini force, one must clear the passage through the central spinal channel, Sushumna, and they do this by the purity of their lives and by means of certain special exercises. This prior cleansing is essential, for when the Serpent Fire awakens it sets in motion every aspect and every level of man's psychic life. The fire is so intense that it consumes everything in its path. It is very important, therefore, to prepare its pathway and clear out all impurities and obstacles so that it may move rapidly up to the Crown Chakra, Sahasrara, without damaging anything on the way.

Do you remember what Jesus said in the Gospels? 'Strive to enter through the narrow gate', and, 'It is easier for a camel to go through the eye of a needle than for a rich man to enter the Kingdom of God.'* The underlying meaning of these two passages is important: what Jesus is saying is that that central channel is so narrow that illumination cannot get through if one's being is not utterly pure and naked. If your pockets bulge with too many possessions you will not be able to squeeze through the narrow entrance: you must begin by getting rid of all your encumbrances. You see: the Indian yogis and the Gospels both proclaim the same truths. And it is these truths that we are striving to grasp in greater depth through the Teaching of the Universal White Brotherhood.

* For further commentary on these two passages, see *New Light on the Gospels,* Chap. 4 (Collection Izvor No. 217)

6

THE CHAKRAS

The Chakra System

I

Where does the tradition of giving Angels wings come from? If you see a painting or sculpture of a winged being you don't need to be told to know that it represents an Angel. But why do we give them wings and what do the wings mean? Do Angels really have wings? No, of course not, but the tradition stems from a very ancient science of man and his subtle centres. The great Initiates of old knew that human beings have two very powerful centres in the back, at shoulder-level. These centres are situated in the etheric and astral bodies and, when they are correctly developed, they create a kind of whirlwind which gives the person the freedom to move through space at will. On the other hand, the tradition of Ancient Greece represented the god Hermes with wings, but his wings were on his heels. This is because there is another powerful centre in the heel which is also related to the ability to move through space.

As a matter of fact, we have a great many of these subtle centres in our bodies. When you are contemplating the rising sun, for instance, you absorb sunlight through a centre which lies just over the spleen. The sun sends us energy in the form of minute luminous spheres and the spleen Chakra absorbs the white light of the sun and breaks it up into the seven colours of the prism, then it sends the different colours to the different parts of the body: red and orange to the sexual organs; yellow to the heart and lungs; green to the stomach, liver, intestines and kidneys; blue to the throat and nose, and purple to the head. Red can also be used to strengthen the nervous system. If someone is suffering from nervous fatigue it means they have a 'red deficiency' and their health would be improved by concentrating on this colour.

The physiological function of the spleen is, as you know, to manufacture red blood cells. It is not surprising, therefore, that the etheric centre of vitality lies over the equivalent physical organ. If you want to absorb these tiny globules of vitality sent by the sun, therefore, remember to concentrate on this Chakra in the mornings, at sunrise, and in that way it will become more receptive and capable of assimilating even more sunlight and you will find that your health will improve and you will have more energy.

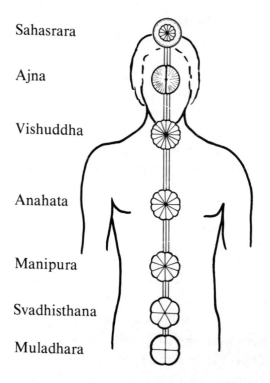

Sahasrara

Ajna

Vishuddha

Anahata

Manipura

Svadhisthana

Muladhara

Figure 8. The Seven Chakras

For centuries, anatomists have been studying the human body, and by observation and dis-
section and with the help of instruments that have
become more and more perfect, they now have an
extremely detailed knowledge of its physical
structure. But for all that they are still very far
from the intimate understanding of man's subtle

anatomy which Initiates have gained through clairvoyance and spiritual experience. And one of the most striking aspects of this is the discovery made by Indian Initiates concerning the seven Chakras of man. For several thousand years now, they have taught that beyond the limits of the physical body, in his etheric and astral bodies, man has a series of subtle force centres lying along the axis of the spine. These centres are called Chakras (a Sanskrit word meaning 'wheel') or lotuses.

In ascending order we have:

— At the base of the spine: Muladhara, the four-petalled lotus;

— Immediately above the sexual organs: Svadhishthana, the six-petalled lotus;

— In the region of the navel and solar plexus: Manipura, the ten-petalled lotus;

— Over the heart: Anahata, the twelve-petalled lotus;

— At the front of the throat: Vishuddha, the sixteen-petalled lotus;

— Between the eyebrows: Ajna, which has two large petals, each divided into forty-eight smaller petals, giving ninety-six in all;

— On the top of the head: Sahasrara, the thousand-petalled lotus. In point of fact Sahasrara has 960 outer petals and a central corolla of twelve petals, which gives 972 petals in all. The twelve petals of the corolla are golden yellow and the outer ring of 960 petals is purple, and the two rings spin in opposite directions.

There is no visible sign of these spiritual centres in the physical body because they are situated in the etheric body. The organs of the physical body, however, are influenced by them.

In the vast majority of human beings, these subtle centres are inactive. In order to stir them to activity a yogi has to awaken the Kundalini force lying dormant at the base of the spine and direct it upwards so that it passes through the Chakras, liberating the potentialities of each one as it goes. Kundalini is represented as a serpent coiled three times on itself inside a triangular form at the heart of the Muladhara Chakra. When it is awakened it is like a flame, a fire leaping up in a spiral movement along the spine, stimulating each Chakra on its way. Tradition says that the Serpent Kundalini uses its tongue to combine and weld together the different elements of each Chakra so that it starts to spin. A Chakra is an extremely fragile system of very fine wheels and only the Serpent Kundalini has the power to set these wheels in motion, and it is only then, when the Chakra begins to spin, that its latent powers and faculties can begin to manifest themselves.

The Chakras all differ from each other in colour and the number of their petals, which means that the frequency and intensity of their vibrations are different, the divinities which dwell in them are different and, above all, on awakening, each bestows different powers and virtues on a human being. Muladhara bestows life force; Svadhishthana, creative powers; Manipura, collective consciousness; Anahata, universal love; Vishuddha, wisdom; Ajna, clairvoyance, and Sahasrara, omnipotence and total freedom. It is said that a divinity or *Shakti* dwells in each Chakra. Their names (in ascending order), are: Dakini, Rakini, Lakini, Kakini, Shakini and Hakini. When Kundalini has completed her ascent through the Chakras, she has reached her goal and is united with Shiva, the masculine principle. As the union of the masculine and feminine principles, the head and tail of the serpent, is consummated, it produces a blinding light and henceforth the yogi has reached the summit, he is totally free.

Hindu literature gives very detailed descriptions of the Chakras, but it would take too long to examine each one, so let me pause, simply, at Anahata, the heart Chakra. It is important for your spiritual development that you carry in your hearts the image of this Chakra which is the centre of Universal Love, for it is this immense, totally disinterested Love which alone is capable of awakening true intelligence in your hearts, the intelligence which we call intuition.

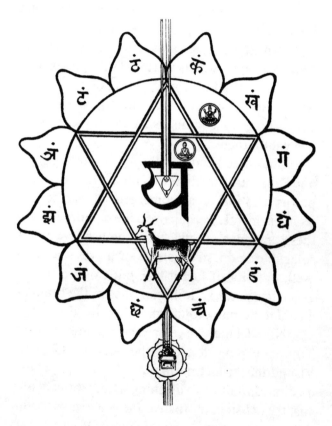

Figure 9. Anahata, the Heart Chakra

An Initiate develops the three Chakras of the head in the last stages of his evolution when every other aspect is ready, when his whole being is harmoniously developed. It may help to give you an idea of the nature and function of these three Chakras if I compare them to three navigational instruments in a submarine: a periscope, an 'eye' which can see above the surface of the water; a radar which warns of the presence of other vessels in the vicinity, and a radio which can receive and emit messages and signals. Human beings have these same instruments, these antennae within them.

The three head Chakras (Vishuddha, Ajna and Sahasrara) are three antennae which the solar plexus uses just as a submerged submarine uses its instruments. Perhaps you are wondering why these antennae are placed in the head; why the solar plexus doesn't have its own eyes and ears. Well, in point of fact it has, but Cosmic Intelligence has placed additional ones in the brain as an aid to human evolution.

Now, let me give you a very simple exercise to help you to develop the throat Chakra, Vishuddha: from time to time, devote your whole meditation simply to listening. Don't think at all. Just try to listen, try to hear the voice of wisdom, the voices of the spirits of light. Of course, at your first attempts you will probably not hear anything, but if you persevere you will eventually hear the Inner Voice, the gentle Voice of God, that voice which is so faint and subtle that it is sometimes called the Voice of Silence. When you hear this voice your whole being will vibrate and tremble — words are powerless to describe the experience.

A method you can use to develop Ajna is to imagine that you are looking with your inner eye at the earth, the sky and the whole of space, with all its countless inhabitants, that you can see all worlds, both visible and invisible. You simply gaze at them with great love: that is all that is necessary to begin to awaken your spiritual vision.

There is also an exercise one can do with the Crown Chakra, Sahasrara, but as it could be dangerous for some of you I shall leave it for another time. The two I have just given you, however, are completely safe: you can start at once and practise them without danger. No harm can ever come to you if you strive to hear the Voice of God. Try to listen, as it were, to your own two ears; in this way it is another, a third ear, which is awakened. Similarly, if you focus your gaze on the wonders of the invisible world, it is your third eye which will be opened.

In this way, step by step, you will travel along this extraordinary path which, if you persevere, will lead you to illumination.

In the Book of Genesis we read that Adam and Eve dwelt in the Garden of Eden in which there were many trees and, amongst them grew the Tree of Life and the Tree of the Knowledge of Good and Evil. God forbade Adam and Eve to eat the fruit of the Tree of the Knowledge of Good and Evil, but the Serpent managed to persuade Eve who, in turn, persuaded Adam, to eat the forbidden fruit — and you all know what happened next!

Well that Tree of the Knowledge of Good and Evil is none other than the series of Chakras lying along the spine, and the Serpent at the foot of the Tree in the Garden of Eden is Kundalini, the Serpent coiled at the base of the spine. The Serpent spoke to Eve, saying, 'If you eat the fruit of this tree (in other words, if you awaken your Chakras), you will become like God, you will be omniscient, clairvoyant and all-powerful.' Well, naturally, Eve was strongly tempted, and Adam too! Yes, but the trouble was that it was premature: they were not ready, not strong enough to contain the tremendous forces involved. They should have been content to go on eating the fruit of the Tree of Life; in other words, they should have been content to go on drawing energies from their solar plexus, through which they were in touch with the whole cosmos, for it was thanks to those energies that they knew nothing of fatigue, suffering or death. Yes, the Tree of Life is the solar plexus whereas that other tree, the Tree of the Knowledge of Good and Evil, is the spine. Adam and Eve were in too much of a hurry to eat of its fruits; they should have waited until God told them that they were ready and could do so without danger.

The situation is exactly the same today: those who know how to draw sustenance through the solar plexus which is in direct communication with the sun, are able to enjoy the fruits of the Tree of Life and to draw on the Prana, the Elixir of Everlasting Life. Whereas those who are in a hurry to eat the fruits of the other Tree before they are sufficiently strong and pure, put themselves in mortal danger. They endeavour to awaken Kundalini, they converse with the Serpent and the Serpent leads them towards death — spiritual death.

Every possible precaution must be taken, therefore, when attempting to awaken not only Kundalini-force, but all the Chakras. I have already given you some simple methods to be used in working with Vishuddha and Ajna, but I should mention another one which applies to all the Chakras, and that is singing. Singing produces waves which cause man's subtle centres to vibrate. Obviously it is not a question of singing just anything or anyhow. If you want to stir your dormant Chakras to wakefulness through song, you must sing profound, mystical songs which produce the right kind of vibrations and you must be conscious, at the same time, of the spiritual forces they represent.

In the Universal White Brotherhood we have a marvellous collection of mystical songs composed by the Master Peter Deunov. If you sing them in the awareness that you are performing a sacred act, some of these songs are capable of awakening in your spinal column a living force which passes up the spine and escapes through the Crown Chakra. Sometimes when you are singing you may feel a thrill flashing up from your feet to your head, a thrill of absolute purity and light: for a brief moment your whole body vibrates in harmony with the universe. Perhaps you have not yet known this blessed experience, or only for a fleeting moment. When you do experience it in all its fulness you will understand the powers and possibilities hidden in song for the development of the spiritual life.

The Chakra System

II

The age-old custom of burning incense or other sweet-smelling substances in churches and temples goes back thousands of years. The smoke spiralling up from a perfume burner symbolizes Kundalini force as it spirals up through the Chakras. The perfume burner containing the glowing coal represents the Chakra Muladhara while the smoke represents the fiery serpent, Kundalini. The symbolism of the perfume burner points to the necessity of feeding the fire with fuel so that the Kundalini force can begin to rise. In spite of having lost the knowledge of its original significance, Christianity has always maintained this tradition of burning incense in church, thereby preserving a rite inherited from the far-distant past.

Figure 10. The Caduceus of Hermes

The secret science of Kundalini can also be found in different forms in several other spiritual traditions. In the traditions of Ancient Greece, for instance, it can be seen in the form of the Caduceus of Hermes with its two serpents twined about a central rod. The two serpents represent Ida and Pingala, the two currents surrounding the spinal channel Sushumna and which yogis trigger into activity by the breathing exercises designed to awaken Kundalini.

In the Cabbalistic tradition, too, we find this science in the Sephirotic Tree with the central Pillar of Equilibrium flanked on either side by the Pillar of Severity (which is positive) and the Pillar of Mercy (which is negative). Two currents flow from the Sephira Kether, one through Chokmah and the other

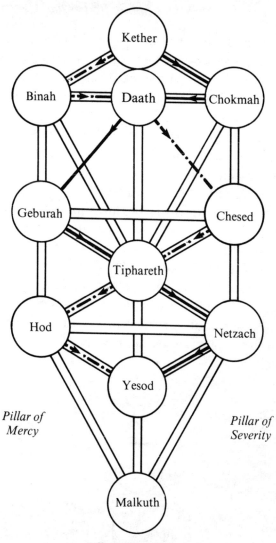

Pillar of Equilibrium
Figure 11. The Cabbalistic Tree of Life

through Binah, they cross over in Daath, pass through Chesed and Geburah, cross back again in Tiphareth, pass through Netzach and Hod and cross once more in Yesod which symbolizes the genital organs.

If you go to Tibet you will see that Tibetan architects have concealed this science of Kundalini and the Chakras in the form they give to the sacred structures called *stupas*. Wherever you go, in the courtyards of shrines and monasteries and along the roads, you will see these structures which are all on the same pattern: a base in the form of a cube; on this cube is a spherical form surmounted by a cone. On top of the cone is a concave form like a bowl or crescent moon, and finally, surmounting the bowl, is a form resembling a flame, a raised thumb or the Hebrew letter Yod:

Figure 12. A Stupa

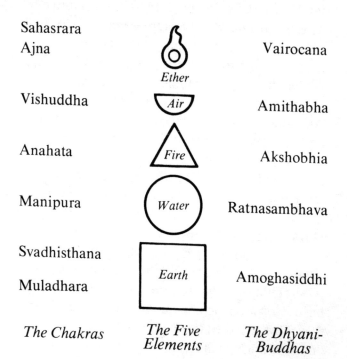

The Chakras	The Five Elements	The Dhyani-Buddhas
Sahasrara Ajna	*Ether*	Vairocana
Vishuddha	*Air*	Amithabha
Anahata	*Fire*	Akshobhia
Manipura	*Water*	Ratnasambhava
Svadhisthana Muladhara	*Earth*	Amoghasiddhi

Figure 13

All the secret science of man and of the universe is concealed in the shape of these structures. The five geometrical shapes correspond, in Tibetan tradition, to the five elements: the cube represents the earth; the sphere represents water; the cone, fire; the semi-circular bowl, air, and the flame, ether. These five forms and five elements correspond, in man, to five Chakras, for the Tibetan system twice combines two Chakras into one. This means that the cube represents both Muladhara and Svadhishthana which are both connected with earth, the densest form of matter. Above these is the umbilical Chakra, Manipura, represented by the spherical form; then comes Anahata, the heart Chakra, represented by the cone or triangle. Above this again is the throat Chakra, Vishuddha, represented by the crescent moon, and crowning the whole is the flame which represents both Ajna and Sahasrara.

Each of these five centres is the home of a Dhyani-Buddha or Buddha of meditation. Their names, beginning with the Buddha of the lowest Chakra, are Amoghasiddhi, Ratnasambhava, Akshobhia, Amithabha and Vairocana. Each one has his own particular quality or virtue, in fact they are also called the Buddhas of the Five Wisdoms, because each virtue is said to be a wisdom.

The five Dhyani-Buddhas are deeply venerated in Tibet, but he who is venerated above all others is the Buddha Avalokiteshvar. The legend recounts that he was the son of Buddha Amithabha and that it was he who, for the very first time, pronounced the sacred formula: OM MANI PADME HUM. The legend also has it that one day he was gazing at the world of human beings, and at the sight of all their suffering and their numberless misfortunes, he was seized by such compassion for men that his head burst into a thousand fragments. Seeing this, his father, Buddha Amithabha, gave him ten new heads in addition to his own and from Avalokiteshvar's body sprang a thousand arms. So now we see Avalokiteshvar represented with eleven heads and a thousand arms, coming to the rescue of human beings.

So there you have a brief description of the way in which the Tibetans, who have received the same teaching about the Chakras as the Hindus, express this teaching in their sacred structures whose forms reflect the structure not only of human beings but of the whole universe.

AJNA AND SAHASRARA

It is important always to keep part of oneself awake. At night, before going to sleep, you should remember to leave someone awake to watch over you while you sleep. Jesus told his disciples to 'Watch and pray', and many people have misunderstood this precept and believed that it referred only to the physical plane, with the result that when the poor things tried to put it into practice and keep nightly vigil, they exhausted themselves struggling against their need for sleep and ended by disrupting the natural rhythms of their body. No, it is on another level that we have to keep watch. At night we must sleep and allow the cells of the body to rest, but at the same time, we must keep watch on the spiritual level, which means that we must keep in touch with the one who never sleeps, the one who watches without pause. Who is this watcher?

Within each one of us, absolutely motion-
less and impassive, is an eternal Watcher who sees
and records everything. Its home is between the
eyebrows, in the Chakra Ajna. Why is it said to be
impassive? Because whatever happens to you it
will never lift a finger to help you. If you are in the
habit of observing what goes on inside you, you
will already have noticed that even in the most
distressing circumstances someone or something
within you sees what is going on and records it
relentlessly, but never intervenes in any way to
help! It is not its job: even when you are suffering
it only smiles. It is no use imploring pity, it simply
looks on, observes, takes note and smiles!

If you want to be vigilant and lucid you
should concentrate, from time to time, on Ajna,
the Chakra between the eyebrows, thus identify-
ing with this eternal Watcher. In this way, even
when you are fast asleep, you remain awake: your
body sleeps but your spirit is watchful and awake
and can travel and meet other creatures and study
the marvels of the universe.

Ajna has been compared to an eye, a crystal
ball or a magic mirror. The virtues of this Chakra
are passive, feminine: it is a mirror in which every
event in the universe is reflected. Ajna can give
you the power to see everything but this does not
mean that you have the power to act: Ajna cannot
give you that. It gives you vision, it allows you to

see images, but it does not allow you to change the course of events or of forces. For this you have to reach the last Chakra, Sahasrara, which is emissive, dynamic and masculine and which can give you the power to act. When the Kundalini force reaches Ajna an Initiate receives a clear vision of reality but he is not yet all-powerful. He is still vulnerable, exposed to antagonistic forces, still tossed to and fro between good and evil. This is why he must attain the crowning point: Sahasrara.

In almost every Hindu temple in India you will see a carved symbol in the form of a flat horizontal stone surmounted by another, vertical stone: this is the Lingam. The horizontal stone represents the feminine principle and the vertical stone, the masculine principle. The Hindu Faithful, men and women, girls and youths, all pray and prostrate themselves in veneration before this symbol, which is often decorated with garlands of flowers, for it is the symbol of generation, of the fertility of men and of gods.

Figure 14. The Lingam

The symbolism of the Lingam is very profound. It indicates that the two principles, masculine and feminine, must not be separated; they must always be united. In human beings, however, they are separated. Men and women are not capable of finding the complementary principle within their own being, they always have to seek it outside themselves and they are in constant torment because they fail to find it or, having found it, remain unfulfilled. But men and women will never find fulfillment if they look for it outside themselves, they can only find it by uniting the two principles within themselves, by being both man and woman at the same time. At that point they no longer need to join themselves externally to another human being with complementary attributes: they are complete in themselves. They possess the wisdom, force and power of man combined with the tenderness, delicacy, purity and sensitivity of woman. In their own person they are a living symbol of the Lingam, they lack nothing and all created things obey them because they are capable of being both emissive and receptive at the same time.

This masculine and feminine polarity can be found in the two Chakras, Ajna and Sahasrara. The horizontal stone, the feminine principle, is Ajna, the Chakra which receives, assimilates and reflects. And the other, the vertical stone, is the masculine principle found in Sahasrara, the active, dynamic, emissive, creative Chakra of the Crown. When an Initiate achieves the union of Ajna and Sahasrara he has reached perfection and is all-powerful: like Shiva he possesses the living Lingam.

By the same author
(translated from the French)

'Complete Works' Collection

Brochures:
New Presentation

Life Lectures on Tape

KC2510An – The Laws of Reincarnation
(Two audio cassettes)

(available in French only)

K 2001 Fr – La science de l'unité
K 2002 Fr – Le bonheur
K 2003 Fr – La vraie beauté
K 2004 Fr – L'éternel printemps
K 2005 Fr – La loi de l'enregistrement
K 2006 Fr – La science de l'éducation
K 2007 Fr – La prière
K 2008 Fr – L'esprit et la matière
K 2009 Fr – Le monde des archétypes
K 2010 Fr – L'importance de l'ambiance
K 2011 Fr – Le yoga de la nutrition
K 2012 Fr – L'aura
K 2013 Fr – Déterminisme et indéterminisme
K 2014 Fr – Les deux natures de l'être humain
K 2015 Fr – Prendre et donner
K 2016 Fr – La véritable vie spirituelle
K 2017 Fr – La mission de l'art
K 2018 Fr – Il faut laisser l'amour véritable se manifester
K 2019 Fr – Comment orienter la Frorce sexuelle
K 2020 Fr – Un haut idéal pour la jeunesse
K 2021 Fr – La réincarnation – Preuves de la réincarnation
dans les Evangiles
K 2022 Fr – La réincarnation – Rien ne se produit par hasard,
une intelligence préside à tout
K 2023 Fr – La réincarnation – L'aura et la réincarnation
K 2024 Fr – La loi de la responsabilité
K 2551 Fr – La réincarnation   (coffret 3 cassettes)
K 2552 Fr – Introduction à l'astrologie initiatique
K 2553 Fr – La méditation   (coffret 3 cassettes)

Editor-Distributor
Editions PROSVETA S.A. - B.P. 12 - 83601 Fréjus Cedex (France)
Tel. 04 94 40 82 41 - Télécopie 04 94 40 80 05

PRINTED IN FRANCE IN NOVEMBER 1997
EDITIONS PROSVETA, Z.I. DU CAPITOU
B.P.12 – 83601 FRÉJUS
FRANCE

– N° d'impression: 2452 –
Dépôt légal: Novembre 1997
Printed in France